JOURNEY

A BICYCLE ODYSSEY THROUGH CENTRAL ASIA

Published by J. D. Huff and Company
1032 Broadway
San Francisco

Library of Congress Cataloging-in-Publication Data

Nichols, Alan Hammond
  Journey : a bicycle odyssey through Central Asia / Alan H.
Nichols. -- 1st ed.
p. cm.
  Includes bibliographical references (p.) and index.
  ISBN 0-9630274-4-1
  1. Nichols, Alan Hammond. 2. Cyclists--United States--Biography.
3. Bicycle touring--Asia, Central. 4. Asia, Central--Description
and travel. I. Title.
GV1051.N5A3 1991
796.6'092--dc20
[B]   *91-27986*

First Edition - October, 1991

Typesetting by Richard Dale Rodrigues

Printed in the United States of America

Table of Contents

pen and ink illustrations by gary goldbeck

1   LOST AT POST 930

The black woman. The nightclub. The dogs. Discolored lumps of fat.
Anger... aching... afraid... sex... Relationships dissolved into
dust. Need... Am I dreaming? How could I be so alone? Is that
why I'm here? Damn it, where am I?

*   *   *

I woke with a start. I knew I was late because it was light outside. I usually rose before the
dawn light appeared. If I started early, before anything else was on the road, I could deal
with the daily quota of bicycle mileage. I was stronger in the early morning and, more
importantly, the wind was weaker.

Strange - the moon's still bright. The chill felt uncomfortable, unsettling. The dry moonscape
was a misty, ghostly gray. Nothing stirred. No birds. No animals. No people.
A time of nothingness - after night, before dawn.

Fearful of being late, I dressed quickly, rolled up my sleeping bag, took down my one-man
mountain tent and got ready to go. To my surprise, after loading my gear into the van, it was
only 3:30 a.m. Because of glass, chuckholes, fast moving trucks and the number of accidents
on this stretch of the road, it wasn't safe to begin riding my bike that early. In the dark a
chuckhole could mean disaster. But I couldn't go back to bed having just spent 45 minutes
packing up.

I climbed into the van, ate a jar of mandarin oranges, some nuts, a Pemmican bar and watched for the dawn, dozing off now and then. It was not the first time I had gotten up too early.

I waited. Finally it was safe to leave. We were on the road to Kashgar. What I needed to do now was ride from a town called Xinhe to a regional headquarters of the Xinjiang Province - Aksu. This was the center of Asia, now the outpost of China's western-most frontiers.

The night before, our van driver seemed vague in describing the next days trip. He told us to take the road to the right when we came to a junction outside the town. But when I got there in the early morning, I felt something was wrong. Just to be sure I asked a couple of local peasants waiting at the crossroads.

"Aksu. Aksu?" I asked, pointing to the right. They shook their heads and pointed left. I thought for a moment, and then turned left. I passed another bicycler and a truck driver; they also confirmed by sign language that I was going in the right direction.

Still unsure, I was relieved when the sun came up behind me, slightly to the south. I knew then that I was riding west; at least I was heading in the right direction.

I pumped hard for about two hours with only a light headwind against me. Keith, with whom I was cycling, left almost an hour later and caught up with me after three hours. We chatted and rode together for a few minutes. Then he sped on by, disappearing over the long desert horizon.

We had to travel 225 kilometers through an isolated, rocky desert area to reach Aksu. We planned to ride 125 kilometers this day and the rest the following day.

As the morning wore on, the sun became a haze behind ever increasing clouds, and the winds began to blow harder. The road was well paved and followed a line of hills to the north. To the south, the rocky plateau was completely flat. The southern horizon seemed to hide the end of the world. Though barren, stark, and dusty, to me the landscape was hauntingly beautiful.

After 11:00 in the morning, I began to get hungry. I was weakening. I had been drinking water from my bike bottles as I rode and had even eaten a few nuts, but it was time for a rest.

Around 11:45, Tang and Chuan, who drove our support vehicle, pulled up and handed me some guava juice, biscuits (really cookies) and some greasy local bread. It was good - almost like a donut without sugar. I also ate a can of sardines, part of a Pemmican bar and a few raisins and nuts. Since it wasn't hot, I was carrying more water than I needed. I wanted to lighten my load and stash one or two of my full water bottles with the truck, but decided against it "in case anything happened." That was one of my better decisions.

The sky became darker and a few drops of rain fell. Chuan asked, "Do you have your raincoat?"

"No, it's not cold and I should be at camp in a couple of hours, so it won't be needed." Just as they were about to drive off, I changed my mind, "Hold it, I will take it." That proved to be another good impulse.

"It's only 20 kilometers," Chuan joked, "see you tonight." Actually, I had about 40 kilometers to go and replied with a smile, "Sure, 6:00 o'clock." That too was supposed to be a joke, since that meant it would take me six hours. I could have walked there in less time.

Soon rain sprinkled the desert. I put on my coat and laid down for a rest. I dozed off, thinking of Mount Kailas - over a thousand miles to the south and one of the main goals of my journey. A change in the wind woke me. It was blowing on my right instead of my left. Previously a headwind, pushing against me, now a delightful gift - a tailwind to carry me forward! I jumped on the bike and began to ride again.

The road was flat with a very slight uphill grade, but the tailwind was helpful. The kilometers, each marked by a numbered cement post, steadily passed by. All distances were marked in kilometers. They were more fun. They went faster than miles and you could do more of them each day.

I was tiring at about the 915 kilometer post. It had been a hard day. It was understood that Keith would pick the campsite around the 920 kilometer post, give or take 10 kilometers in either direction depending upon terrain, wind, weather, suitable places to camp, etc. Usually Chuan or the van would wait by the road to direct me to the exact camp location.

At Post 915 I began searching. At 920 there was still no sign of them. I was surprised because I didn't think Keith would go further that day. All afternoon I had pedaled across a rocky plateau on a narrow paved road with a slight roll every two kilometers. I was tired because of the now steadily rising headwinds.

Also by, Post 915, the terrain started to become hilly. Gullies and outcrops appeared at Post 920. I decided to go the agreed ten more kilometers. A dry wash at Post 923 had a number of possible camping places, but there was no sign of the others. There were no tire tracks or possible side roads. I went on to Post 925. Now I was getting anxious, and they were still not in sight.

At Post 926 a large tank truck stopped ahead of me. The driver and a passenger got out and waited for me. Then a sexily dressed Chinese woman with a red skirt, high heels and a lacey white blouse got out too. She was sure a surprise. They all smiled as I rode up and by gestures offered me and my bike a ride. "Aksu?" I asked. They nodded agreement. I think the woman said, "What's kooking?" Her smile, bright red lipstick and encouragement were tempting, but I had to find my companions. I smiled, then said, in very poor Chinese, "Dubushay. Sheah. Sheah." (Sorry. Thank you. Thank you.)

I rode on. They soon passed me with a few honks and some friendly smiles and waves. I felt totally alone as their truck disappeared over a hill.

By Post 927 I became very worried. Road workers were doing something about a mile off the highway in the desert. Could our van be stuck out there? No, it wasn't there. I went further to, Post 930, even though the area was less promising for campsites. I got to Post 930 at 3:38 p.m. No one was there.

Every instinct I had was to move - forward or back, anywhere. But if I went ahead and they were behind, they might never find me, since they would figure I would probably not go beyond Post 930. But if I backtracked, I would drain what little energy I had left.

The prospect of staying on the desert alone all night scared me. I was now frantic. Could some disaster have befallen them? I had to wait at least two hours. Maybe I could have passed them without seeing the camp or maybe they didn't expect me so soon and didn't leave Chuan or the car by the road. They might still find me. If not, there was almost enough time and light to ride on to Aksu. I Knew I'd feel better with a little rest anyway.

I got to Post 930 at 3:30 p.m.
No one was there

The weather was erratic - now it was very hot. I drank almost all the remainder of my water. My near panic was matched by the changes in weather. The sky grew dark. Heavy black cumulus clouds began rolling over the hills from the southwest. Drops of rain fell, and I heard distant thunder. Lightning flashed a long way off. The thunder was soon overhead. The hills to the south turned a whitish grey in the mist - it was impossible to tell if it was snow or white dust.

I began watching for vehicles, becoming more and more upset. Trucks would appear on the horizon to the east and over a hill to the west. At a distance some looked like our van - white with a blue tarp over the roof rack. For a moment, when I thought it was our van, I was immensely relieved. The feeling turned to panic as the vehicles roared past me. To calm down, I stopped watching and laid down for a while in the ditch beside Post 930 trying to rest. It became harder and harder to sit still as the minutes passed. I tried meditating for a while. Then I climbed a hill to see if I could spot a camp. There was nothing but more hills and rock.

At 5:30 p.m. I decided to wait another hour. I ate the rest of my food. The possibility of making it to Aksu decreased with each darkening minute. By 6:00 o'clock, I decided I had to try for Aksu. Either they were ahead of me, or something had happened and they couldn't look for me. Perhaps the overloaded springs of the truck had collapsed off the highway. Maybe a bad road accident that was cleaned up before I had arrived. Possibly the camp stove had blown up. I was at least two and a half hours overdue. In that time, they could have driven back to my lunch stop post and forward to Post 930. Perhaps Chuan had taken my 6 p.m. joke literally. It was possible, but, if so, they wouldn't start looking for me until well after 6:30. They would probably retrace the route first, so they wouldn't find me until eight. Being out that late was risky. Aksu would be impossible to reach in daylight if they didn't show up. "Thank God, I kept my raincoat," I told myself.

I held back and told myself I would ride to Aksu at 6:23. There was no particular reason for the odd time. I began my ride to Aksu at exactly 30 seconds after 6:23.

After about 30 minutes, I realized how little reserve energy I had. A truck loaded with sacks of corn passed me and stopped. The driver, a clean-cut young man with a mustache and a bright red sleeveless T-shirt, gestured as if he wanted to give me a ride. I hesitated, then asked, "Aksu?"

He nodded. I readily accepted my hoped for salvation.

The driver helped me load my bike onto the grain. Another young man got out of the cab and sat with me on top of the load. Two older men, with traditional box like hats, gave us their wool coats. The rain started to pour and the wind blew. It was cold, but I wasn't uncomfortable, thanks to the old man's coat and my own raincoat. It felt wonderful to be moving. The two of us huddled together on top of the corn sacks against the storm. As the hills and the kilometers passed, I knew I never could have made it to Aksu without the lift.

My plan was to find the police or the China Mountaineering Association representative in Aksu and go back to Post 930 to look for the expedition. Just as I began to relax and the storm abated, the truck stopped at Post 971. I knew Aksu was still 50 to 60 kilometers away.

The driver got out, pointed at me and to his feet and moved his feet up and down. I knew he meant I was to get out. I was confused. I stalled. Then I started to get my bike but he shook his head "No." He pointed up the road. His gestures (a circle around his upper arm meaning an arm band and police or army and a stiff arm up or down meaning road block) told me what I had to do. The young man on the load, with me and one of the two other passengers in the cab, disembarked.

They wanted me to walk through the roadblock, leaving my bike on the truck. My passport and what little money I had were on that bike in a bag attached to the handle bars. I was helpless if they left me without my bike. Dare I put so much trust in complete strangers? (My Klein mountain bike would bring a small fortune on the black market.) To gain time, I pretended I didn't understand. But I needed the ride. I was desperate. It was getting dark.

I got down from the truck, pretended to note the license number (I noticed they all smiled at that) and walked straight ahead around the curve in the road and through the road block. The army and the police were there but didn't stop me. I walked fast. The truck with my bike passed me and rounded the next curve out of my sight. My heart sank. I was alone with no passport, no money, at this remote roadstop.

I ran around that curve down the road. The truck was there waiting. I was on top of the world!. I climbed back on top of the corn sacks, grateful beyond measure.

We arrived at the driver's warehouse in Aksu. The driver and I shook hands. He couldn't help me any more. People crowded around, so I was afraid to pay him. That was the right thing to do, since I later learned drivers aren't supposed to pick up passengers and especially are not supposed to receive money for it.

I walked into a street crowded with people, bikes, trucks, donkey carts - everyone was on the move. Aksu is not a tiny hamlet but a city of 100,000 people. There were no police or anyone that looked approachable. I couldn't ask my way. I didn't even know what to ask. Talk about a language barrier. I said, "May gwok [America]," with gestures out of my mouth trying to mean "Can you speak American?" This didn't work. My driver's armband gesture meaning police was equally nonproductive. I tried putting my hands together on the side of my face as if sleeping. A man pushing a cart apparently caught the message and pointed out a large building half a block up the street.

I thought it was a Chinese hotel, with scores of young Chinese boys in soccer uniforms in the parking lot. Local onlookers crowded around me and my bicycle. I gestured, smiled, looked anxious (that came naturally), but they only stared back.

Finally, two bright looking, nicely dressed men rescued me. Neither spoke English. I showed them the calling card from Madame Lu Ming, Chairman of the Sports Committee in Urumchi - that seemed to help. I also showed them a page of my notebook with the name (in Chinese) of the Aksu China Mountaineering Association representative. That didn't help at all.

One man picked up the telephone and the other guided me and my bike into a waiting room where there was some control over the number of gawkers. By gestures, I understood one of the men was going to drive somewhere and get me some help.

I was glad to be somewhere, but as time passed I wondered if I had been abandoned. I would survive, but more importantly, what had happened to Keith, Tang and Chuan? Two hours later, a small middle-aged lady with large glasses, well dressed in a tan jacket and skirt, entered the reception area.

She said something like "hotel." I was so overjoyed to find someone who spoke English that I burst out with my story until I realized she didn't understand a word I said. The gist of our conversational gestures became clear: I was to follow her to a hotel and was to leave town for Korla the next morning. I wasn't able to get the point over that I had already been to Korla and was going to Kashgar, the opposite direction. And she didn't understand anything of my need to find the police to locate my lost companions. She led me on her bicycle to the hotel, showed me a room and disappeared.

One hotel worker gave me a document to fill out asking for my passport. I wrote "passport in van," even though I had it with me. I hoped that my not having papers would bring the police or an army translator It didn't work. My lady "interpreter" came back and gestured I was to follow her again. We headed across a large courtyard toward an old impressive building. Maybe it was the police or army headquarters. But it was only a dining hall where I was given a late dinner. I ate, feeling guilty that I had a place to stay and food without knowing what had happened to the rest of the expedition.

After dinner, I walked back across the courtyard. To my shock, in front of the hotel was our van! We all greeted each other with mild recriminations but mostly with smiles and joy. They had stopped at Post 917 and set up camp but missed me when I passed. It seemed so simple, and yet ...

2 BEGINNINGS

My meeting on Kowloon had been cancelled. So I rushed to make an earlier ferry back to Hong Kong. It took some frantic footwork to squeeze through the closing ferry gate, but I made it. I then decided to go out on the upper deck for a breather...

A stranger approached me. A well-groomed young man, mid-twenties maybe. "My name is Keith Brown, you a mountaineer?"

Odd question. I'm not dressed in a way that would cause him to ask that. What did he want? I'm curious. So I talked with him.

That's how it began.

Without giving me a chance to react or even wonder why he picked me to talk to, he took out a small binder from his briefcase and showed me pictures of Celestial Peak, a spectacular pyramid-type mountain in the Sichuan Province of western China. He was on his way to try a solo climb.

In less than ten minutes, the boat ride was over. We walked off the boat and continued for a block or so. During the walk he told me he had just received a permit for a unique expedition. He was to be the first person to cross the Gobi and the Taklamaton Desert and the width of Tibet from west to east by bicycle. No one had done it before.

I was impressed, "What an adventure!"

"Would you be interested?"

"Sure."

He took my business card. We parted. He seemed a nice guy, but I didn't think anything would come of it.

Months later, after I had almost forgotten the meeting, I received a letter from him.

* * *

Dear Mr. Nichols:

I'm writing you about the Xinjiang-Tibet Mountain Bike Expedition we briefly discussed on the Star Ferry in Hong Kong. The China authorities have given me full permission and I am now raising funds and planning the specifics of the trip.

I've enclosed a sponsorship prospectus and map, but want to elaborate on some of the details.

aa)   Permission is granted for 110 days and allows cycling of the full route as indicated on the map, across Xinjiang and Tibet. The section of road from Shiquanhe-(Mt. Kailas)-Saga is prone to mud slides, but if open, will be used rather than the north Tibet route shown on the map.

bb) The Chinese were adamant the cyclists must have a support vehicle and refused to give permission without [it]. A support vehicle certainly increases the chance of success and offers some interesting possibilities for photography, side trips, etc.

cc) Permission also allows the expedition to take several days off from cycling and circumnavigate on foot the sacred mountain Kailas.

dd) Photography enroute is unrestricted.

ee) The China fee is US$10,000 (ten thousand dollars) PER PERSON, in addition to a registration fee of US$2,000 (two thousand dollars). The fee includes cost of support vehicle and driver, food, air fare Beijing/Urumqi-Chengdu/Beijing...all costs within China.

If you are interested in the trip, I'd like to know your position on the following:

//Can you contribute or help raise funding for myself?

//If I have secured funding can you secure US$10,000 for yourself?

//Do you want to cycle the route or are you interested in riding in the support vehicle (having a trip member ride in the support vehicle has not yet been discussed with the Chinese)?

//Do you have 110 days to ramble around Central Asia?

I was impressed by your interest in sacred mountains and also give my respect for your athletic tenacity (Western States 100). I think you could be a good choice as a partner for the Xinjiang-Tibet bike trip. So please let me know your interest!

I send my best wishes.

Sincerely,

Keith Brown

I was flattered to have been asked. But it was impossible. The bicycling was obviously over my head. And I suspected my sponsorship was more important than my participation.

But I wanted to go. Sure the rationale said I'm 56 years old, the sole caretaker of an eight year old, and have a law practice that needs me... And for what? To get myself killed trying to keep up with a 26 year old? To travel to the middle of nowhere? Why? Because I wanted to and more, importantly, because I felt I needed to.

While I might not have known it at the time, I also wanted to be free of all the confines of my world, a sabbatical from life as I knew it. The adventure sure, but there has to be more for a man well into his fifties to risk his life and livelihood. The seed of that Had begun ten years earlier...

* * *

In the mid-seventies I had reached a dead end. Fortunately I had no idea how long that dead end would last. For, had I known, I would have found life unbearable. My life appeared, on the surface, to have been the fulfillment of the American dream. I had a successful law practice, was married, had two children, and was active in local politics. It had taken a long time, but my marriage had begun to fall apart - maybe it should never have been. What looked to be so great on the surface covered a relationship in which two people had nothing in common. Then I ran for public office and lost. Under most circumstances I would have bounced back easily, but since I was already feeling hurt and isolated, I took it a lot harder.

Then into my life came a truly despicable woman. No man likes to think that a woman has no interest in him other than for her own personal gain. This was her motive. I was not and am not a wealthy man, but then a wealthy man might have been more wary of women like her. But, considering the level she was looking up from, I must have looked like the golden goose.

I was a fool. I probably knew what came out of her mouth was nothing but lies, but I didn't want to admit it. I was pathetically lonely. I remember days and days of coming home from work, my wife off on another of her social climbing efforts, my kids off doing their thing, and me left with a note and a plate of food in the refrigerator for dinner. Part of it was my own fault. I wanted the perfect family, where everyone behaved perfection, and were just crazy about each other. Because they didn't fit my concepts of perfection I resented them, and because I didn't fit their concepts of husband or father, they resented me. With my involvement with another woman, what had been a shaky marriage ended.

I'm a very good lawyer. In fact, I'm great at resolving conflicts between other people, but I'm terrible at managing endless demands and tantrums in my personal life. With my wife and this other woman at loggerheads, I ended up being maneuvered out of my own home and ended up living with a nightmare. The nightmare became pregnant and had my son. If I thought I had problems with my wife, it was nothing compared to this new hell I found myself in. I continued to live with her because I could not abandon my responsibility to my child. She didn't particularly like Shan once she realized he wasn't going to produce a wedding ring that was to give her access to community property. I hated her, but I wasn't too pleased with me for getting myself into this trap. I traveled as much as possible on business to get away from her. But she was so awful that even as an infant Shan couldn't stand her. I stayed home more and more - he needed my protection. So even that avenue to escape was denied me.

My fantasy world took over and offered me some solace. I was so lonely and isolated that when I traveled I wrote many letters, beautiful letters. Letters to a loving family waiting for me in a happy home. I wrote to the woman in my dreams hoping against hope that when I returned to San Francisco what I dreamed would be reality. As I approached my house, in dread, those hopes were always dashed.

Any thought of further involvement with politics or public service died. I didn't dare risk the

21

scandal. She threatened to disappear with Shan if I refused to support this arrangement. I was trapped.

So life became hell. I couldn't leave because I had to protect Shan from her violent temper and hysteria. I feared for my clients and my business and the people who earned their living based on that business. I was so ashamed of this woman, yet I couldn't get rid of her.

Then a miracle happened. She found another man and wanted to leave. They were going to make fortunes together. This fortune was going to be made from the seed money obtained from me as a payoff for custody of Shan. I would have sold my soul to get rid of her. and I came close to having to, but it would have been worth a hundred times the money.

In those years I had become a social cripple. I had few friends outside my office and I had no life aside from Shan. There was little sense of purpose or hope and no future. I was so used to living in a state of constant anxiety I didn't know what to do to get started again once I was free.

The few friends I had were wonderful. They invited me out, set me up with dates, did everything they could. Yet I still drifted. I desperately wanted to do something - to feel alive again! Now was the time, maybe this trip would be my chance. All sorts of wonderful dreams began to take hold...

Just think of it. To be the first in the world to do something! Could it be that in me lived the spirit of Marco Polo, Admiral Perry, or Sven Hedin? The thought of it was a magic carpet of realizable dreams. My magic carpet was to be a bicycle. Twenty-two pounds of aluminum, rubber and steel - perhaps not as exotic as camel caravans or dog sleds - but I will power my craft. I will carry an Explorer's Club flag to the ends of the earth. I will do something no one has done before!

I sent my reply...

Dear Keith:

Thank you for your letter. You probably didn't remember (or I didn't mention it) that my objective after Hua Shan in China was Kangrimpoche (Kailas) in Tibet. I was the first white foreigner to circumambulate it last May (although Hedin probably rode [a horse] around the mountain in the 19th century).

The whole idea is very appealing. My only reluctance is my 8 year old son. I would hate to leave him that long. Here are my ideas:

Be sure we control the places we stop at night. They always want to stay in villages, but I've found being out in the open is much cleaner and healthier. (On my trip to Mt. Kailas the villages were the only places I got sick.)

I would want to cycle, not ride, but the available transportation is an excellent addition in case of injury or just to take a day off now and then.

I can raise $10,000.00 for my share if you can raise your $10,000.00 . . .

I'm a member of the Explorers Club (New York), and we might get some support if we carried their flag (no obligation except to "carry the flag" with a picture probably on the Dolma La).

Any ideas about bike type, equipment, food, etc., that presumably the Chinese won't furnish?

In short, if you're still interested, count me in. If the Chinese agree, then I'll get to work on the project.

Best regards,

Alan

My first responsibility was my son. His hesitations about my taking the trip were dispelled by a promised trip to Disney World when I returned, a postcard or some communication every day, and a time capsule made by the two of us to bury in Tibet. In addition, while I was gone, a cattle drive with his older brother, and a summer at our cabin at Fallen Leaf Lake in the Sierra Nevadas with his aunt, her children and his grandmother.

I found from my conversations with my partners that I wasn't as vital to the law firm as I had anticipated, so suspending my life for awhile seemed less threatening and permanent. The disappointment of discovering my dispensability was overcome by the relief of my guilt feelings at planning to be gone so long. This was to be a time for me.

Now that I knew I would go, I gorged on maps. I love maps. They release the floodgates of my imagination. Maps of this area have always overwhelmed me with their vast distances, strange sounding names and mystical associations. I found a large-scale Bartholomew World Travel map of China and Mongolia that presented an overview of the whole journey. It was easy to trace the route since there was only one road on the map. I found out later that maps of Central Asia are sometimes more the products of imagination than reality. But for the present I let maps feed my dreams.

The prospect of cycling directly into the heart of Asia thrilled me. The Gobi, Kashgar, Lhasa, Yarkant, the Kun Luns, Tibet and the Himalayas along our route were to me the epitome of adventure, history, and mysticism. We would bicycle in the footsteps of Genghis Khan and along the Silk Route to China. Here in Central Asia was the interface of the greatest power struggles and intrigues of the world, past and present, between the ancient civilizations of China, India, Russia, and many others.

How I dreamed of my journey to this center of the world, our planet's largest land mass (17 million square miles). It was here that the Moghul Khans gathered their horde to invade China, the Middle East and Europe. Our route was to be through the historic gateway to

Tibet. A land that was never opened for any foreigner but the Chinese, Indian pilgrims, and for a brief moment, to the British Army during their invasion in 1904. We were to travel the only road along the borders of some of the most disputed territories in current history. Here were the Russians against the Chinese (our hosts, the Peoples Liberation Army - PLA), the Indians against the PLA, the Pakistanis on alert from all sides (Russians, Indians and Chinese), and the Afghans locked in their own struggles. On this same corridor of movement, Alexander the Great's troops still cast their long shadow. Finally, our way was also the way of Buddha, as this was the route used by his followers to spread his message of life from India to the Moghuls, to the Chinese, and finally to Japan.

I wanted to see this area before the inevitable hordes of tourists changed it and made it commonplace. I wanted to join the soldiers, priests, traders, and thousands of people seeking adventure over countless years by crossing this transition corridor of the history of man's cultures, religions, and peoples.

The route we planned would cross the mountainous Tian Shan twice.

The first 6000 miles from San Francisco to Beijing would be standard air travel. Keith said he would meet me in Urumchi, where our trip was to begin. Urumchi was China's western most capital and the government and army headquarters of the Xinjiang region near the Russian border.

Keith and I wanted to make history by being the first to cycle the road from Urumchi to Toulapon, and from Toulapon west to Kashgar in Xinjiang. The route we planned would cross the mountainous Tian Shan twice, and then along the Taklamaton Desert, a part of the fabled Gobi so long integrally associated with a source of world terror - the Mogul armies of history. After Kashgar, we would have to head south along the Pamir Mountains bordering Russia, through the Kun Lun Range and the Korakoram Mountains, followed by journeying through the Aksai Chin, still actively disputed territory between India and China. Finally we would take the old pilgrim route from the westernmost border of Tibet by way of Mount Kailas east to Lhasa, Tibet's capital.

I was overjoyed to think I could again go through areas of Tibet and China seldom seen by westerners in modern times and never before bicycled by anyone. Foreigners had never been allowed, on bicycles or anything else, in the highly sensitive military areas between Yeching and western China, and Mount Kailas in western Tibet. Finally, it would be the first time a cyclist had ever made the 3,300-mile journey through both Xinjiang and Tibet, or from Urumchi to Lhasa.

As I delved into charts, books, weather maps, and other literature, I realized our only chance to complete the trip would be if we began very early in May and finished in early August. Without some unusual intervention by forces beyond even the Peoples Liberation Army and China's Chairman Deng, the season for travel was too short for the distances we had to cover. We would have to be at the right place at the right time or fail.

If we were too late going through the Taklamaton Desert (part of the Gobi), we would be fried in the 135 degree heat. I was warned the road temperatures would be 175 degrees and could melt our bicycle tires. Yet if we went too soon to avoid the desert heat, we would get to the Kun Lun Mountains too early and be buried in snow on the passes. In the Aksai Chin, we might freeze in the minus 30 degree winter temperatures of this coldest place on earth. Or if we were late, we risked being bogged down in mud in the valleys of the Korakoram, the Kun Lun, and the Aksai Chin. And on the last section of the journey, if the snows of the Himalayas and the Trans-Himalayas (Gangdise Shan) melted before we had crossed most of western Tibet, the annual floods would either drown us or leave us stranded on a Tibetan hillside.

It was much later that the consequences of these uncertainties dawned on me. If we misjudged the weather or our cycling speed, we might be stranded for days, weeks, or even months. It could mean we could go neither forward nor retreat home. Mountains, deserts, and impassible country would be both behind us and ahead of us. But in my euphoria, none of this mattered.

We would have to average at least 40 miles a day of cycling to cover the distance within the time limit of weather and Keith's permit. I had never ridden that many miles in one day, let alone day after day. All the bike touring books that I bought repeated the advice, "On a long bike tour, you should ride half the distance each day that you normally ride on a one-day trip." At that rate, I would have been as old as the mountains by the time I finished the trip. But these calculations and realities weren't able to interrupt my dreams of breezing through Xinjiang and Tibet.

People die trying to be first at some physical feat, but pilgrims are notoriously lucky getting where they want to go. On this journey I was to be a pilgrim. My identification with this area and the explorers of its past became almost a religious fervor. To me Mount Kailas was more a spiritual experience than a mountain. I had been there before, now I wanted to return to this sacred place. Only this time on my own power. I wanted to circle the mountain again and the sacred lake below. If I did this, I sensed I would truly discover that a spirit of life lived inside me - one full of laughter, joy, hope and adventure.

3 PLANNING AND GOING

For two months Keith and I exchanged long telexes about sponsors, supplies and the ever continuing discussions with the Chinese. Keith had accomplished the impossible - a written expedition agreement with China's governmental agency, the China Mountaineering Association. We later discovered what every lawyer already knows, there is always room for more negotiation. And Chinese officials are the consummate experts.

In late February, Keith, on leave from his work in China, flew to visit his family in New York and Virginia. On the way he stopped in San Francisco, so we had a chance to meet again. I picked him up at the airport and we spent the day together. Our mutual enthusiasm for adventure clouded the obvious fact we were a mismatch.

An experienced biker, intense, in his twenties and in superb shape, Keith was completely dedicated to the success of what he called "The Expedition." He had some mountaineering experience but had never led an expedition. For him this was no lark but serious business. A stickler for details and exactness, he was well organized, highly motivated but virtually humorless. He would be difficult to know. Would he risk too much to accomplish his goal? Would we have fun? This was clear, he would lead. The question was, could I follow? I have always needed to be in control. It made being shy and insecure easier to handle. I could hide the pain - but criticism and failure were always devastating. Now I was putting myself to a real test.

We both wanted to overlook the discrepancy in our ages, physical condition, cycling knowledge, objectives and feelings. When I asked, "Do you think I can keep up? I'm afraid I'll slow you down." He told me that he'd thought about that but, "You finished the Western State Endurance race [a 24-hour, 100 mile footrace over the Sierras] the year before last. You can keep up with me."

We spent the rest of the day together, talking about the various potential sponsors. We decided who was to contact each of them for support of the expedition. After taking him to the airport, I was feeling both enthusiastic about the trip and doubtful about how I would perform.

* * *

In two months I was to be on a plane to Beijing. There was barely enough time to dream about it. Yet I knew the anticipation might be more enjoyable than the experience. I had sixty days to button up my life, to put everything on hold and in order.

I hedged against injuries and serious illness - medical testing, prescriptions, immunizations, even a new will. Any spare moments were spent gazing at maps of the places we were going to or in reading about the areas. I'm afraid the books on Tantric Buddhism proved easier to absorb than those about bike maintenance. Assembling and packing equipment and supplies seemed to be an overwhelming job, so I happily put those tasks off.

One of Keith's last telexes reminded me not to forget a visa. I had forgotten. Without it the Chinese would have sent me back. The rush to remedy this oversight added to the excitement. I anxiously wondered whether there was anything equally vital that I might have forgotten.

Several sponsors of the expedition from Hong Kong and the United States gave us bike parts, bike clothing, and bike shoes. I had all the latest gear for cycling but nothing to ride. Trusting that it would all work out, I continued to contact sponsors.

Though not forgotten, I was missing the critical ingredient for a cycling trip: a bicycle.

A friend and cycling expert, George Bach-y-rita, helped me look for a touring bike. Some seemed too expensive, others didn't fit. I just couldn't bring myself to buy a bike at all. There was no question, I couldn't cycle through Central Asia on a heavy one-speed Chinese bike. Keith wrote about the need for extra wheels and referred to mountain bikes. Up to then I had been looking at touring bikes. The lighter, small tired, touring bike could never have carried me through the mud and dirt over the passes and across the rivers beyond Kashgar.

The bicycle dilemma was solved by Mountain Bike Specialists in Fort Collins, Colorado. They told us they would give us the latest high-tech aluminum frame (very lightweight) Kline mountain bikes. We were to test the bikes on the rough terrain of Central Asia to find out how much punishment they could take. I was delighted. I also stopped shopping.

Less than 30 days before leaving, I received my bike. What a thrill! The blue high tone, large, but light framed machine seemed to smile at me. At least I know I smiled at it. I told it, "We're going to be a long time together, taking care of each other and coming home with you as an heirloom."

I had planned many training rides on my new bike to get used to it and to be fit for the journey. I knew the stress would be beyond anything I had experienced. But I was so overwhelmed by all the other needs pressing in on me, I couldn't find the time. So I settled for a few trips across the Golden Gate Bridge to Marin County parks. The bicycle was better than I deserved. I felt like a commuter driving an Aston Martin to work.

But the bicycle did begin training me: how to shift, brake, oil the chain, etc. While I never had a flat tire over years of riding, the lugged bicycle tires went flat twice in a month. It was a struggle to fix them, especially the rear one. I developed a passion for avoiding flats - to dodge every piece of glass I saw, to wipe the tires off often and to keep them properly inflated. These were lessons that would help in the months to come.

The mountain bike was superb. I grew to love it. It was ready to go to China with just a last minute overhaul. But it couldn't do anything about its rider. I wasn't ready. "After all," I rationalized, "I'll have a few weeks on the road to Kashgar from Urumchi to prepare my legs and lungs for the mountains and Tibet."

The last two weeks before departure were hectic. I did a lot of last minute shopping in response to Keith's telexes from Hong Kong. It also became apparent that there was nowhere to buy anything once the trip began. New sleeping bags, special sunglasses and rain gear, as well as extra film, arrived only a week before leaving. Every new package added to the excitement.

I was sure the Explorers Club in New York would like us to carry their flag, a flag that has been used for over 50 years by other adventurers. As a member of their club, I wrote them a couple of weeks before we left offering to take the flag. The Club requires a precise "scientific purpose." Our purpose was to be a study of blood lipids . . . mine. I had been part of a blood fat intervention research project at Stanford Medical School. The trip provided an unusual opportunity to test some of the hypotheses about exercise and diet. It turned out to be more of a test than we planned. But this project required a last minute flurry of tests and meetings with the principal investigators, John Farqhuar, M.D. at Stanford Medical School Heart Disease Prevention Dept. and Charles Rudy, Ph.D., biochemist and nutritionist.

As a result of my conversations with Drs. Rudy and Farqhuar, I took along every medicine, herb, vitamin, food supplement, and concoction either of them prescribed, whether traditional, experimental or simply esoteric. I had something for every illness, injury, disease, nutritional need, special situation (altitude or cold, for example) and every conceivable symptom. These supplements were an answer to every hypochondriac's prayer and health nut's delight.

The piles in my living room grew daily. So did my anxieties. Would I get sick? Be injured? Could I really make it?

But stronger voices whispered, "I will be free. I will ride with the wind and sun surrounded by history. I will be alone in Central Asia, responsible to no one. My own body, my will, my emotions will harmonize my whole being. I will do what no one has ever done before."

With only 36 hours before departure everything was still in a huge pile in my living room. To pack it all in one night would be impossible. My bike was still not back from the shop from its final overhaul. . . Panic.

Like an angel filled with good humor and cheer, my law partner, Dan Rapaport, convinced me there was nothing more I could do. He said the office was ready for the extra workload while I was gone. And, with the help of my office staff, in six hours on the night before departure, we packed the four file boxes each with Pemmican bars, dried fruits, canned tuna, salmon, chicken and sardines, nuts and dried tomatoes. Most of the canned fruit and vegetables, grains, camping mixes, and powders just had to be left behind. There was no more room. We also filled a huge suitcase with all the medicines, herbs, and food supplements and packed all the camping gear. I said my thanks and good-byes to them all hoping they wouldn't notice the tears in my eyes.

Shan helped too. It was a good excuse to stay up late and look at all my "neat stuff." Around 10 p.m., Shan and I were alone. We drove to an all-night drug store to buy some missing supplies. I had given him $50.00 for his own to use while I was gone. Knowing I would be alone and that I loved classical music, he insisted on using most of it to buy me a Walkman tape player. I was deeply touched.

At midnight the bike shop owner arrived with my bike and helped me pack it. We strapped it as one piece in a huge box. For protection we packed the cold weather gear I was taking along around it.

Departure day. I loaded up all the gear into my old station wagon. My other law partner, Steve Doi, along with two other people from the office, drove with their loads of supplies to the airport. Shan and I rode buried in the gear in the station wagon. My stomach churned. I was excited, nervous, and filled with anticipation.

The public relations director for Japan Airlines, which provided our air transportation, met us at the airport. He was extremely gracious, but even I could tell he was appalled at the sheer volume of stuff! There were 18 separate items of baggage: a huge bike box, a box of extra bike wheels, a large duffel bag, a suitcase of medical supplies, four boxes of food supplements, another first aid supply box, five equipment boxes including camping gear, bike parts, extra tires, film and photography equipment and a miscellaneous box of supplies, etc., etc., etc...

He was too polite to complain, but did manage to ask, "Will you bring this much back?"

He seemed relieved when I told him, "We'll eat, wear out and throw out most of this on the way so there'll only be me, hopefully, and the bike, for sure, to come home."

Concerned with the baggage overload and needing to keep some things with me, I wore two coats (a heavy down jacket and a raincoat), carried a Hassleblaad camera, a Nikon F3, one of the video cameras, with batteries and tape, a toiletries kit for the way, and a briefcase of files, papers and maps. I was a caricature of one of those people you desperately hope will not sit next to you on an airplane.

During those last few minutes, a surge of gratefulness swept over me. I thanked, hugged, and shook hands or kissed everyone who was there to see me off. As I went through the last checkpoint for passengers only, I could feel the tears welling in my eyes. The enormity of the journey suddenly struck me. What was I doing? Why did I inflict such pain on myself? I felt so alone and stupid. I looked for my mother, who was with my son, for one last wave, but by then they were gone.

I sat in a waiting area for a few minutes. Gradually new thoughts came to mind. I was healthy, I was free, without cares, and on my way to an adventure of the ages. I was sure I would return happier, wiser and more at peace with myself.

When I heard, "Last call to board Japan Airlines Flight 1 to Tokyo," I was ready to go. Sometime before I had adopted Milarepa, a Tibetan Boddhisattva, known as the "Laughing Teacher," as my patron saint. Behind the sounds of that boarding announcement, I could swear I heard Milarepa's encouraging laughter.

Keith and I and our now 25 boxes, three bicycles and several bags flew to Urumchi.

4 NEGOTIATING FOR TOMORROW

There was a slight change in plans and Keith met me at the Beijing Airport when I arrived from Japan. He had been in Beijing for several days and had re-confirmed all the permits we needed for the expedition. Just to be on the safe side we both met with the Chinese representatives of our sponsoring governmental organization, the China Moutaineering Association. Our trip was confirmed. We were told that as a matter of form we had a new sponsor, the China International Sports Committee, another governmental agency. We had no idea that the change would pose any problems. After two days of meeting with officials, Keith and I and our now 25 boxes, three bicycles and several bags flew to Urumchi.

It was a beautiful day. I was intrigued by our flight of only a few hours by jet over hundreds of miles of the wastelands of Western China. I knew that the same trip by caravan reported by Marco Polo, Sven Hedin and other adventurers took months. Our plane landed at the small but modern Urumchi Airport. We disembarked onto the runway into a warm clear afternoon. The desert air was crisp and fresh. I was exhilarated.

We were first met by Amanda, Keith's friend and business associate. She had helped with Keith's negotiations in Beijing for the necessary permits and, to my surprise, was going to travel with us in our support vehicle for two or three weeks. Keith said her knowledge of Chinese would be very helpful.

Immediately after we met Amanda, a young man surrounded by several other young men approached us. With a smile, he introduced himself as the Urumchi Branch Manager of the China Moutaineering Association. His entourage included our assigned liaison officer, Officer Tang, and our translator, Mr. Chuan.

Right after the preliminaries, the Branch Manager, still smiling and cheery, announced, "You'll have to return to Beijing on tomorrow morning's plane. You don't have the right permits."

We were shocked. Our first reaction was to "politely" express anger. "There's no way we're going back," we said, "we're leaving tomorrow by bicycle." But the manager's announcement had the desired effect in negotiation rituals - it made us very uneasy.

The prospect of starting over at Beijing kept us quiet about other complaints we had. We didn't dare say anything about our less than desirable accommodations at the "Oilman's Hotel" in dusty, smoggy, noisy, downtown Urumchi. The "real" tourists stayed in new bungalows nestled in a forest of poplar trees on the outskirts of town. Of course we weren't supposed to be tourists. It was deemed our piles of boxes, bike parts, all weather clothing, camping gear, water jugs and supplies were more appropriate to the bustle of the Oilman's Hotel, our "expedition headquarters." For our "untidy" piles would have jarred the serenity and well organized hospitality for foreign guests in the bungalows.

The next stage of the negotiations ritual opened on our first evening in Urumchi. To keep us in the game, we were told we did not have to go back to Beijing but could wait in Urumchi for the new permits. In fact, we could begin our journey as soon as they received a critical telephone call from Beijing "tomorrow." We were optimistic. There was nothing else we could do, so we agreed on "tomorrow."

Meanwhile, perfect bicycle weather was going to waste - clear, little wind, morning temperatures in the mid 60's. We wondered how long it would hold before the dust storms, the scorching heat and the winds common to the Gobi and the Taklamaton Desert returned.

"Tomorrow" was spent waiting all day to hear about the telephone call. We used the day to check our route out of town, rearrange gear and see the countryside. The terrain outside Urumchi, irrigated fields surrounded by bleak deserts and mountains, reminded me of Idaho and the intermountain west of the United States where I grew up.

Urumchi is the provincial capital of western China and the Xinjiang Autonomous Region. The entire region has only thirteen million people (Shanghai alone has the same number and China itself a billion) but it represents 20% of China's land surface. Except for downtown Urumchi and a few scattered villages and towns, the region contains millions of acres of wide vast open spaces, mostly barren deserts and mountains. The area is dominated by the ever increasing numbers of immigrant Chinese from China proper (now 44% of the population). There are thirteen distinct nationalities in this region including Ugyurs, Moguls, Tartars and even Russians.

Xinjiang was once the northern focal point of the Silk Road, an ancient link to the rest of the world that predated recorded history. The Silk Road is so named because of its role over the last 2000 years as the route for transporting silk and other luxury items to India, the Middle East and Europe from China. It was also the way that Buddhism was brought to China and the way eastern elements of religion were brought to the Middle East. The religions of the Silk Road worked themselves into the doctrines of Zoroastrianism, Christianity and Islam.

Marco Polo stopped in Urumchi. In the manner of the George Washington refrain, everyone claims, "Marco slept here." If so, Mr. Polo undoubtedly spent many hours in the negotiations ritual before being permitted to proceed on his history making journeys in the 13th Century. No wonder it took him 26 years to complete his trip.

This area is important to China agriculturally. It is also critical to China geopolitically. Within a few miles of our planned bike route, Russia and China maintain over a million battle-ready troops along their borders. A war raged in Afghanistan. Pakistan's soldiers nervously guard their border. And India, still smarting from her defeat by the Chinese army, has thousands of her best troops in readiness. The area between Ladak (part of India) and China still remains "disputed territory." The road we must take goes right through it.

It is not surprising that China would be reluctant to upset this balance of power in Central Asia by allowing two potentially politically troublesome American cyclists to pedal through such sensitive areas. Who could be sure the Russians, Afghans, Pakistanis or Indians would not want to claim jurisdiction over us! In this corner of the world they fight over very small things.

The rumors of the negotiations vacillated between hopeful and discouraging. On our second night in Urumchi the negotiations were led by the branch manager supported by an associate, the translator and our liaison officer. Pursuant to an understanding Keith and I had worked out earlier, Keith spoke for us. The negotiations between the Branch Manager and Keith proceeded (roughly summarized, based on what their translator said):

"You can't go without a central government approval," the branch manager stated.

"But you said we already have it now," Keith replied.

"No. You have a travel visa and permit, but you need a special permit."

"But this trip has been planned for a year and was officially approved in January and April of this year."

"But we need another permit."

"Then get one."

"We can't guarantee it, but we will try."

At this point in the ritual, the traveler is expected to be upset, angry, contrite, appreciative and demanding. We were!

The manager suggested we wait to hear from Beijing and see the sights in the meantime. In a show of orneriness I demanded a vehicle to take us to Heavenly Lake in the Altai Mountains a hundred miles away.

"It's no use," they replied, "the lake is frozen with ice two to three meters thick."

"We want to go anyway," Keith rejoined

It was our turn for a victory, so they agreed.

* * *

After turning off the main highway (two lanes, paved but bumpy as if the desert had been paved over "as is"), we headed up into the Altai Mountains for about 20 miles on a rough gravel road. Heavenly Lake lies about 3000 feet higher than the desert. We were told that according to an ancient legend, a goddess bathed there because the lake was so beautiful. Thus, the "wash basin" became heavenly. We didn't ask how old "ancient" was, but the legendary bath must have been fairly recent because I found, upon inspecting the outlet that the "lake" is really a reservoir finished less than 20 years ago.

Nonetheless, the large misty vale above the lake proves other-world beauties once did exist here - a sparkling alpine stream, green meadows, waterfalls guarded by sharp cliffs and ridges crowned with pine and huge dragon spruce trees.

The smell of pine and the fresh cold water were an exquisite contrast to the desert only a few miles below. And above it all 18,000 foot snow-capped Mt. Bogda, known as "the mountain of the father's eyes," seemed to gaze down with a dazzling brilliance from its snow light, brighter than the sun itself in a blue sky. We celebrated with a swim in the icy waters of what the driver called Mini Heavenly Lake.

The tourist season had not yet begun at Heavenly Lake, but ten huge tourist boats and scores of small boats at the dock confirmed the complaint by a local guide that the lake was overrun with boats in the season.

When we returned to our hotel, the liaison officer told us it was time to discuss "this whole matter." This was preceded by a statement that we couldn't leave Urumchi, but we couldn't remain at the hotel either, because a long stay was not included in our prepaid fee. A perfect dilemma. And we knew it wasn't a mistranslation because the translator good humoredly acknowledged the incongruity.

We met in a large room on the top floor of the hotel. When we arrived, their team was already seated in a row on one side of the room. They gestured us to seats across the room. I didn't sit down but broke the pattern and moved to their side. We sat on large, light pink overstuffed couches and chairs, all with white doilies on the arms and backs.

The talk went on for two and a half hours. By the end we had all changed seats, but nothing else had changed. It was late. We were tired and tense. The Chinese team was personally accommodating but seemed oblivious to our anxieties. The whole trip seemed to be falling apart over the technicalities of the permits. The delays alone could make the journey impossible as the weather got hotter and windier on the desert. Keith and I talked alone and decided to just go without a permit.

The Manager stood firm, "You are not allowed to go . . . yet."

"But you now have the Beijing approval," Keith reiterated.

"Yes, but we don't have the document itself," the Manager retorted.

"How soon can you get it?" I chimed in.

"We have a call in now to Beijing."

During further discussion into the reasons for all this, the manager left the room to "take his call to Beijing" (at 10:30 at night). He returned and reported, "We now have the document we need in Beijing."

We sat on large, pink overstuffed couches and chairs, all with white doilies on the arms and backs.

"Good. We'll go in the morning." Keith replied.

"You can't."

"Why?"

"Because the document hasn't been chopped [stamped] yet."

"When will that happen?"

"Tomorrow."

"Then we'll go the next day?" I said

"No, we have to receive the document and that can take ten days."

"That's impossible," we both protested, "we'll leave anyway."

By this time, someone's apparent objective, whatever it was, had been reached. We felt sure we would never go, and between ourselves, started thinking about how to get our money back. Desperate, we began to suggest alternatives.

Keith opened our new approach, "You say you have all approvals, so it's only a matter of paperwork. We'll leave for Toulapon and you can bring the document to us since we will travel only fifty miles a day, at first anyway."

"No, sorry."

"Why?"

"You can't get by the security checkpoints on the way to Toulapon."

"Why not?"

"You won't have your passports."

"Why not?"

"Because we will have them."

"Give us a letter that you have them, and we will use that to get through the checkpoints."

"We can't."

"We'll just take our chances on being turned back."

"We can't."

"What if we skipped Toulapon and took an alternate route through the Tian Shan [the mountains to the south]?"

"You can't. The road is closed."

The room was silent. Keith had been stonewalled, so I continued, "When can we leave?"

"We will get the chop tomorrow and then get clearance here."

"Then we can leave the next day?"

"We can't guarantee that."

Predictably, there was a new surge of anger from our side.

"This trip was approved months ago! Why all this hassle?"
(Again there was a long silence.)

"Then someone made an error?" I guessed.

"Yes."

"Why?" Keith pursued.

"Because of the confusion. You were initially sponsored by the China Mountaineering Association and now by the China International Sports Association."

"That's the only reason?"

"Yes."

Somehow this confession of error made us all feel better. Maybe there was a chance we would be allowed to go if the only problem was inter-agency coordination.

We never found out why they didn't receive our special permit months earlier from Beijing. But understandably our whole journey made them nervous. They were surprised we really had a permit to do what we claimed. The reason became clear. We were to be the first foreigners (or Chinese for that matter) to travel by bicycle through the areas planned. Like most other bureaucracies, the Chinese always react with extreme caution to "firsts." We were to pass through three provinces and several military zones. We were class D travelers going into areas that were off limits to foreigners. Even our government liaison officer and translator needed special permits to go with us although they did not need them to accompany other classes of foreigners. China is broken down by areas for travel, such as class A (open, unrestricted areas), class B (foreigner's special permit areas) and class C (no foreigners without special approvals). Class D areas are prohibited to foreigners and Chinese except on special, usually military, business.

Even though we were exasperated, they always appeared to be accommodating, as if they regretted having to say no. It was an improvement over many western bureaucracies, who seem to delight in saying no, politely or otherwise. The next day - another "tomorrow" - we were escorted to several places on the tourist lists, including the local friendship store. We declined to visit the arts and crafts pavilion. The provincial museum and the exhibition hall (where they held nightly "disco" dances for the local young people) were huge. The army exhibits in the museum were better put together than the others and included multi-media, computer-controlled battle scenes. Most tourists missed this exhibit because it's a long walk to the third floor.

After dinner that night, Tang told us to meet again in the negotiating room. Their whole team was there looking relaxed and the manager was smiling. He told us proudly,

"We have the document number and don't need the document itself."

"Then we can go tomorrow?" Keith asked

"No."

"Why?"

"Since we don't have the document, we need a local official to verify on another document that you have the security approval from Beijing but not the document itself."

"When will that happen?"

"Tomorrow."

"When?"

"In the morning."

"Then we can go in the afternoon?"

"Maybe."

I stood up and toasted the manager with a glass of coca cola. We all laughed. But the gesture was premature. By noon on that "tomorrow" he had no document.

The ritual was finally coming to a climax. Our after lunch meeting on this latest "tomorrow" was a volatile one with questions of trust, confidence and deceit floating in the air. It concluded with a promise by the manager to find the official to sign immediately provided we drop our insistence on accompanying him to meet with the official. We were to content ourselves with a call to the Beijing manager of the China Mountaineering Association.

After waiting for a report for two hours, Keith and I went for a bike ride. We ended up at a hilltop fire station. The firemen were playing basketball, so we invited ourselves to join them. Everyone, including scores of spectators, enjoyed themselves. When we arrived back at the Oilman's Hotel, sweaty and dirty, the manager met us.

"Please come immediately," he said, "the Chairman has been waiting a long time for you."

We rushed up to the third floor conference room for the finale of the Urumchi Ritual. We knew the meeting would be formal whether we were told we could proceed or must return to Beijing. A very tall, overweight woman with piercing narrow eyes came to meet us as we entered the room. Though friendly, she spoke only to Keith as the leader and explained the dangers and the responsibilities of the journey since it had never been attempted before.

But she smiled. We then knew. We smiled.

The permit read:

>*"Keith Brown and Alan Hammond Nichols are authorized to travel by bicycle in all restricted areas along the route from Urumchi to Kashgar to Lhasa subject to applicable security regulations. Signed The Chairman, Xinjiang Autonomous Region."*

The last "tomorrow" had arrived. We left Urumchi the next morning.

5 HIGHS AND LOWS

The last of the delays were over. Madame Chairman returned to bid us farewell. We met one floor down from the negotiating room. The couches this time were brown leather.

Our political stars had risen. The whole Sports Committee of the Xinjiang Region plus the China Mountaineering Association staff were present. Our mutual thanks, statements of the friendship, handshakes and smiles, etc., were covered by still and movie cameramen and were broadcast throughout China by television and radio. The whole committee shook hands with us and all had their pictures taken several times.

Madame Chairman was clearly the leader. Her committee included an Ugyur native obviously uncomfortable with the honor, a friendly young giant seven feet tall, very heavy, who modestly admitted he was a basketball player, a Shanghai colonial who had been in Urumchi for 25 years and a mountain climber.

Madame Chairman focused on me this time so I concluded that her avoiding my eyes in the prior negotiations was not a matter of protocol but a stiff neck.

After another set of pictures in front of the hotel and our van, we finally mounted our bikes and headed out of town. Behind and ahead of us were cameramen and press people recording our beginning. I was dressed in my best sponsor-furnished bicycle togs. People waved and called to us as we cycled through the city. A few miles out of town the euphoria of publicity began to melt in the noon-day sun. Our extra CMA escorts and the TV cameraman returned to town. We were finally alone on the road. I took off my fancy cycling jacket and helmet and put on my own "gear" - an old white dress shirt and a tennis hat with a cloth napkin sewed down the back. I did keep on my long turquoise riding pants to protect my legs from the burning sun. The real journey had finally begun.

We climbed a small pass and coasted down the other side into the Jaggar Basin of the Gobi. The day was clear and hot. A headwind, light at first, blew heavier as I sweated through the long afternoon. I had complained the day before that the 90 kilometers (about 54 miles) Keith planned to ride to the next town was too far for the first day, but the driver drove the sag wagon (van) to a town much farther, so I had no choice but to keep pedaling. I caught up with our van in Dabancheng about 7:30 that evening. I was totally exhausted. I was also a little uncomfortable about my companions' apparent disregard for me.

Our Chinese "motel" in Dabancheng had dirt floors, dirt walls, and dust covered everything. But the natural thatched roof kept it cool. I was so tired, and my stomach had started feeling queasy, I didn't dare eat the proposed native dinner of rice, fly-covered meat and vegetables; instead, I found some crabapples and peanuts in a local indoor peasant's produce market. The driver also bought some "champagne" for me. It was bottled and purportedly contained some alcohol, making it safer to drink. It had a slight orange taste and was delicious. Needing all the liquids possible to reverse my dehydration, I drank two quarts of the champagne with no noticeable effect. At least I don't remember any special effects . . . except an overwhelming desire to sleep.

I didn't sleep well. The room's dust settled in my nose and lungs making it difficult to breathe. The flies seemed to stay active all night. I got up with the pre-dawn light, put on

The road headed down into a canyon. The air was cool with the morning dew. There was no dust, no traffic, no one else.

my cycling clothes, ate a piece of bread from my saddlebags and went out of the compound onto the highway. I knew Keith and the others would follow in a few hours. From the first moment, that ride became a cyclist's dream.

The sun was rising behind the mountains to the southeast. The road headed down into a canyon. The air was cool with the morning dew. There was no dust, no traffic, no one else. The downhill grade, with a nudge from a tailwind, sent me skimming over the asphalt surface at 20 miles an hour. Pedaling was unnecessary - I only had to watch out for potholes. I yodeled and sang to the river that plunged alongside. Echoes bounced off the dark grey and black cliffs all around. The valley was hemmed in by sharp rocks and carved mountains whose ridges dropped straight to the river. Now and then a patch of morning sun would slant through a side valley on the river and the green willows. It made the water sparkle. I had planned to stop and eat some prunes for breakfast after an hour of riding, but I couldn't - the ride was much too exhilarating even to slow down. This was the joy, freedom and oneness with the world I had dreamed!

Finally the canyon widened and a large plain came into view. I decided to stop and savor the soaring canyon ride. Although the road was almost flat, I had to squeeze my hand brakes very hard to stop my bike. I turned around to look back up the valley. To my surprise I found myself and my bike flat on the ground. The wind was so strong it blew me and my bike into a ditch. Unhurt, and after recovering from the shock, I remained on the ground, drank some water and ate a piece of bread.

I couldn't get back on the bike. After a while I figured out that by turning my back to the wind and jumping on the bike quickly I was able to resume the ride. The wind caught me and sent me sailing out on to an enormous treeless rock-filled plain. Although the speed was frightening at first, after a few minutes I became confident that the bike could take the rough road and I could steer it around the potholes. I took my hands off the brakes and just let the wind push from behind. It blew me south and east at 35 miles an hour over the flat plateau. Loaded trucks coming the other way against the wind labored in their lowest gears as if they were going up a steep grade.

I flew past a fork to the left in the road. For a split second I considered turning, "Could this have been the turn off to our destination, Toulapon?" The road seemed too small to be the way to that famous ancient city in the desert, and there was no road sign. I had hesitated too long - the wind carried me quickly by the junction making it impossible to stop or turn. Anyway, I was having too much fun.

About ten kilometers beyond the turnoff, the road headed south. I knew then that I was going the wrong way. I decided to try to find somewhere out of the wind to wait for the van. But I also knew stopping could be perilous. I slammed on the brakes as hard as I could and jumped off. The wind blew the bike out of my hand and stunned me. I managed to pick up the bike and push it into a roadside ditch and lay down next to it.

An hour passed. No Keith, no truck. It would have been impossible to ride against the wind back to the turnoff. It was doubtful the wind would decrease. In fact it would probably be stronger in the afternoon. I knew I could ride about 30 kilometers to the south, to Tocsun, a small village, and wait. But there I would be alone with nowhere to stay or eat. From my experience it is better when in trouble to save your energy by waiting. That's also the hardest to do when you are anxious. But I did wait. To my great relief, an hour later Keith appeared above my ditch.

After a few words shouted over the wind, we decided to go on together to Tocsun. We sped like eagles. In less than an hour, we came to another fork in the road. According to the map, the road to the left should intersect the highway to Toulapon about 30 kilometers away. To confirm that my map was correct, I stopped a bus and Keith talked to some villagers.

Our ride to the north and east involved bucking headwinds and crosswinds. It was torture. The same winds that had made me laugh were now the enemy. They sapped my energy and sucked nearly every drop of moisture from my body. Keith went on ahead because I was so slow.

The driver of the van found me but the vehicle was already overloaded so they could not give me a ride. I tried to ride alongside the van using it as a windshield, but they could not adjust to my speed and went on ahead. I fell further and further behind. Soon I was alone with the heat and the wind. Everything was sore - legs, lungs, rear end, arms, neck. I drank all the water I had (five bottles) and was still desperately thirsty. I could actually feel my whole body dehydrating. Finally, after a couple of hours I saw a building and a crossroad that had to be the junction to Toulapon. But every time I looked up it seemed to be the same distance away. Was I truly riding so slowly? Everything shimmered in the heat waves, unmoved by the hot gale winds.

I finally made it to the crossroads. Keith and the van were waiting by an old adobe building. We had lunch inside. Then we rode the wind south, followed by some easier pedaling over a

I was fascinated by Toulapon and embarked on a morning of exploration.

flat paved road with a crosswind on the eastern leg of the highway to Toulapon. That night I slept a bit better. I was fascinated by Toulapon and embarked on a morning of exploration.

Toulapon had been an important city on the 4000 mile long northern Silk Route that brought gunpowder, the art of paper making and printing, and silk from Xian, China's capital to Europe. Such trade was first recorded in the records of the Han Dynasty, 206 B.C. to 220 A.D.

We took the van to Jiohe, the 2000 year old ancient capital of the Che Shi Kingdom. Its crumbling mud walls and staircases were only a hint of its former glories as bastion of priests and lords of the land.

For me the climax of the tour was Baizeklik, the Thousand Buddha Caves, a huge solitary Buddhist monastery carved into the desert cliffs miles from any populated areas. The whole area, now deserted, retained its spirituality in spite of centures of vandalism. First by Muslims defacing the Buddhist symbols, the by Europeans who took statues, icons and even pieces of the murals on the walls, and lastly by the Red Guards who destroyed the hundreds of images of Buddha painted on the cave walls.

By afternoon, the queasy feeling in my stomach had turned into severe cramps. I also had a 102 degree fever as well as the first signs of diarrhea. I delved into the cache of medicine I had brought along to see if anything would help. After dosing myself with selected items, I just passed out.

The next morning was impossible. There was just no way I could ride. I could barely even wake up. I couldn't believe we were only three days into the journey. Keith acquiesced to one day of rest - then we had to move on.

It was so heavy the shocks
were inverted and the van looked
like an overstuffed mushroom.

6 DEVIL WIND

Things were getting bad. I was sick and weak. Every muscle in my body ached. It was hot.
The winds constantly blew against us. And we had over 3,000 miles to go. All my fantasies
and dreams were turning into nightmares.

Keith was discouraged with me. He was feeling strong and wanted to keep moving.
Although he agreed to an extra rest day for me in Toulopan, the delay made him very
nervous and irritable. I felt guilty holding us up.   We were already late starting because of
the negotiations in Urumchi. Used to leading and toughing it out, I was upset with myself
for being the cause of more delay. Keith suggested that he go ahead and that I rent a second
vehicle in order to catch up with him. But I wanted to attempt to cycle all the way as much
as he did. In any event, feeling at least able to move after my day of rest, I started out early
the next morning to our next destination.

There was no room in the van for me or my bike, since Amanda was riding in it for the first
two weeks. The driver constantly complained about the overloaded vehicle. Our van actually
waddled down the road. It was so heavy the shocks were inverted and the van looked like an
overstuffed mushroom. Every cranny was filled. Five feet of boxes were on top and the

three occupants were so buried in the baggage that it looked as if no one was driving.

As difficult as it was, I wasn't ready to give up almost before we began. For the next week I rode on my ego. I would do it or die. Something inside drove me on as if my life was at issue. I could not let myself fail. My credo - that I (or anyone else) could do whatever I set out to do - was at stake. Failure here would prove that the rationale for this whole trip and in fact this whole concept of life was wrong.

I was angry, "Keith, the Chinese, this highway, can't beat me - I will make it." Yet I was afraid the journey was too much for me, especially in my poor condition.

My law partner, Dan, used to tease about the fact that, "Alan's idea of an outing is that everyone starts out to do some activity and when everyone collapses except Alan, the activity is over." It was meant as a joke, but now I was starting to realize that for the others who took part with me in these "activities" it might not have been as funny.

Possibly those hikes or camping trips or ball games could have been more fun if I had accepted the pace at which others operated. I couldn't figure out what was "wrong" with them, just as Keith couldn't figure out what was "wrong" with me. Maybe I shouldn't be so hard on myself and those around me by thinking failures are the result of not being good enough or not trying hard enough. I will push myself as hard as I can. I will give it all I have - but if I don't manage to finish the trip, it doesn't mean I'm a failure as a human being. There are impossible standards - and I have to learn to accept that - that they are impossible.

Cycling from Toulopan to an army camp in Tocsun confirmed my fears that things could actually get worse. The early morning began pleasantly enough - an overcast sky and almost cool. By nine in the morning the weather had become muggy, hot and windy. By 9:30 the road turned from the south to the west towards the Tian Shan, the first mountains we were to cross. The same gale winds that days before had blown from behind us blew head on this time. I couldn't ride forward at all. I was furious - it seemed a personal affront to me. I screamed at the wind. That didn't help. It only blew harder. "The wind flowing from the Gobi is personally after me," I thought. Then I remembered the admonition I read, "It's hard

to enter the Gobi. But if you're strong enough to enter, you'll never be strong enough to leave."

My first instinct was to jump off my bike, sit down and wait for someone to turn off the damn wind. So I did. Keith came back a few paces to me and said, "The wind could get worse, get going."

That thought brought me to my feet but the wind blew my bike so I couldn't hold it steady. I tried to jump on the seat and pedal in my lowest "granny gear". It worked for a moment. Then I realized I wasn't even moving enough to keep from falling over. To my amazement Keith jumped on his bike and made forward progress against the gale. "Had he sold his soul to the wind devil?" I thought as I watched him ride further and further away to the west while I seemed to be pedaling backwards. I could actually feel myself drying out and my temperature rising. I was already tired and the day had just begun.

Keith was able not only to stay on his bike but move ahead. He waited for me a few miles up. Necessity resolved my problem. If the wind wouldn't let the bike carry me it couldn't stop me from carrying the bike. I bowed my body against the wind with my head on the seat and pushed the bike. In a couple of hours I finally caught up with Keith. He shouted over the wind, "It is easier to ride than push the bike. Just get on."

"Are you kidding? I can't even walk. I'll meet you in Tocsun. Go ahead."

"Okay," he shouted, then he left.

After a few more miles of staggering I knew I should return the two hundred kilometers to Urumchi, but I could see all the "I told you so's." Anyway Urumchi was more upwind than Tocsun. I decided to go a little further and sit out the wind no matter how long it lasted.

I then came to the crossroad going south. The gale became a crosswind with a touch of tailwind on some stretches. In less than a minute my tormentor became my booster. The rest of the day's ride to Tocsun army camp was easy.

Without knowing it I rode right by our night's stop at the Tocsun Army Base and twenty kilometers out into the desert. Chuan, our translator, had been posted at the Army camp to watch for me and show me where to turn off the main road. He got bored with such a dull assignment and was diverted by watching the girls passing by on the road. I was angry, but much later I conceded he may have been the only one with the right sense of priorities.

After a night in the army barracks, I was on the road again early in the morning. Although strong winds came up occasionally, especially in the afternoons, the gale left us. But it wasn't until after we struggled over the Tian Shan's Dry Valley Pass from Tocsun into the Taklamaton Desert.

As each day of the journey passed, more of my pretenses were dissolved. I came to realize that there are bicyclists and there are cyclists. Cyclists are an elite and I am not one of that elite. But I also found that as miserable as I was, I did have some sense of humor left.

I came to the conclusion that cyclists were mutants. They never tired. Back home they spent their days riding, chatting at bike shops and reading cycling magazines. They didn't do things normal people do. They didn't get sore muscles and never had sore rear ends.

Cyclists also know all about bikes. In preparation for the journey, I bought several bike repair books. They were full of philosophy, physics, metallurgy and technology. That was understandable - it was the "how to" explanations that got me. The step-by-step directions for repairing or even adjusting my derailleurs or rear spring brakes made taking the bar exam seem easy. Flat tires were hell. The rear tire proved to be especially troublesome - the chain would get stuck and I couldn't get the damn "fork" into those two "notches." Why can't the bicycle industry understand this? The industry has also obviously never pumped a 65-pound-per-square-inch mountain bike tire by hand. I could never get the stupid pump to move after 50 pounds. Real cyclists don't seem to have these problems.

I don't know what God thought about all this, but I had the suspicion Milarepa was on my side - in spite of the chuckholes, sharp rocks, debris, and green glass from beer bottles all over the roads in Asia, I didn't have a single flat tire. For someone who hated changing tires as much as I did, that certainly brought joyous laughter.

It was foolish of me to attempt a 3,300 mile bike trip. This type of trip is not for amateurs that are out of shape and don't know what they're doing, and I was an amateur. But I still clung to the belief that there was a special place in the world for pilgrims and dreamers. I had said I was to be a pilgrim. Pilgrimages can be tests of faith and courage and character. Maybe this will get better. In the meantime, the big question for me in the Xinjian Autonomous Region deep in the heart of West China on the road to Kashgar was not, "Will we make the 3,300 miles from Urumchi to Lhasa," the big question was "will I make it the next 175 miles to Korla where I'm told I can have a day's rest?"

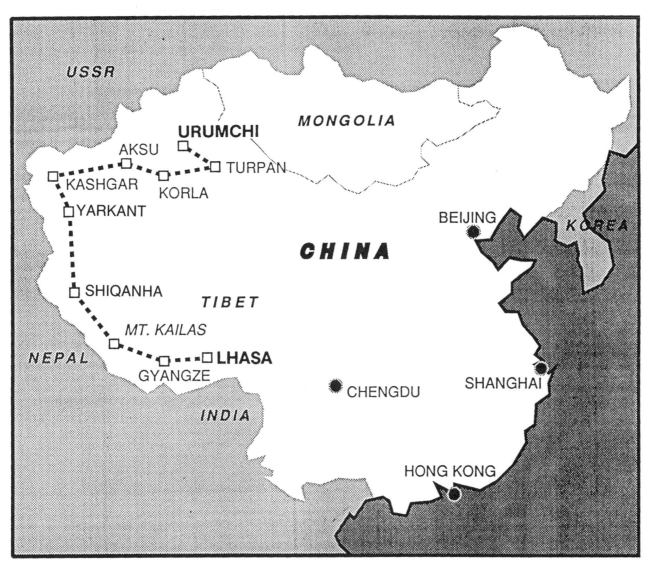

The Expedition's route.

Nako Tso, a lake near the
Xinjiang - Tibetan border.
"The mountains are power.
The lakes are peace."

Market and fair on the Silk Route, southern Xinjiang. "He who sells horses to a horse trader has more skill than a matchmaker."

Dentist at Yarkant - last chance for teeth cleaning for 2000 miles.

"There is more beauty in a stone
than in a hard hearted woman."
People's Liberation Army camp in the Akasi Chin

Author at Wild Goat Pass,
Karakoram mountains.

Keith "phoning home" from Kashgar
on the latest equipment - no cord needed.

My camel may be stupid, ornery and ugly,
but she keeps me alive so I love her."
In the Kun Lun mountains.

"You can destroy the picture but never the image,
destroy the home but never the message,
destroy the Holy Man, but never the soul."
Thousand Buddha Cave near Toulapon.

Mohammed said, "Pray and you shall be rewarded,
Pray five times a day, and you shall see heaven."
Id Kah Mosque, Kashgar.

"Many a man and woman die from their thirst."
Lemonade stand at an oasis in the Taklamaton Desert.

7 DRY VALLEY PASS

To Keith, Tocsun to Korla was be just a warm-up. To me it was a survival test. To our driver and translator it was a chance to see if these strange Americans were smart enough to quit before they got started. For the expedition this was a chance to get to know each other. Only to Keith's friend, Amanda, was it a vacation.

While my combination of potions didn't cure me, they did make it possible for me to ride - sort of. Whatever I ate soon left me. What I had was diarrhea elevated to an art form. I didn't think it was possible to feel this sick and miserable and survive. I would soil myself and, without having a change of clothing or a means of cleaning with me and with the relentless need to keep going, I would just keep pedaling for hours in my own filth.

Patterns of personal interactions were developing. These did not bode well for the trip. I decided I did not like Keith personally, although I had great respect for him as a cyclist. I also became uncomfortable and suspicious about just who Tang and Chuan were and exactly what their roles were.

On the day we left Tocsun we had to cross our first major pass over the Tian Shan Mountains. I came to call it Dry Valley Pass even though it didn't officially have a name. I left the army base at Tocsun alone early in the morning. I was told we were to camp with tents somewhere on the way up the pass before the afternoons winds picked up.

Keith caught up with me by 10:30 in the morning. We rode together for awhile across a flat rocky plain on the approach to the Pass. Keith showed me how to catch a ride on a passing truck. He would spot a slow moving truck, get behind it, increase his own speed pedaling furiously, grab the tailgate and hang on. "Hey, that's cheating," I thought - we were supposed to be cycling the whole way. My second thought was, "This was dangerous." But as we cycled into the foothills and the grades became longer and steeper, my third thought was, "What a great idea."

A slower than usual truck was coming up from behind. I stood up on my pedals and pumping as fast as I could as the truck passed I grabbed the chain on the right rear of the truck bed. I held on. The truck sped up on the flat area and swerved toward the shoulder. My front wheel wiggled back and forth. Just as I was about to lose control I let go. My left arm hurt from holding onto the truck even for that short time.

hitching was still easier than pumping so I caught another truck and held on...

Struggling under my own power, I soon decided that hitching was still easier than pumping so I caught another truck and held on for several kilometers. My arm ached as if it were coming out of its socket - it probably was. The pavement suddenly ended and the truck plunged into the gravel potholed road in a blinding cloud of dust. My front wheel hit a hole, my bike flew into the air in one direction, and by good fortune, I flew in the other. Except for a good scare and skinned elbows, I was uninjured and the bike apparently didn't mind the flight at all. However, I told myself, "No more free rides."

It wasn't until after the adrenaline wore off that I realized I was shaking from the cold wind that swept down from the higher parts of the Pass. Riding was impossible so I huddled behind a rock to wait for the van, aware as time went on that I was very thirsty and had no water left. It was now afternoon, the van was late and I was worried. "At least," I thought, "as soon as the van gets here we can select a campsite." The hope of water and rest settled me. Keith whom I had passed on my free ride, now pedaled past me.

The sky became darker and more overcast. It was too cold to stay still so I decided to go ahead. I tried to ride but the grade was too steep for me in my state so I pushed my bike up the hills. When the road leveled off a little I began to ride again. The late afternoon headwinds were cold and I was becoming angry at how inconsiderate my companions were.

"Where the hell is the van? What are they doing? Why haven't they got here to set up camp? Don't they know I'm sick? How far are we going today?"

What I didn't know was that they planned to go all the way over the Pass into the desert and many more miles to Kumix Army camp. They weren't planning to camp on the pass at all. They had deliberately lied to me.

In spite of the cold, hunger and exhaustion, my anger at the realization I had been lied to gave me enough extra energy to keep pedaling. Trucks kept on going by, each covering me in another layer of dust. About 5:30 in the afternoon a large blue dump truck roared by. Through the dust I could see its taillights go on. The truck finally braked to a stop about 200 yards ahead. The trucker, a young man with a very friendly smile, jumped out and beckoned to me.

I'm afraid I was not a joy to behold. "What do you want?" I asked.

He replied in Chinese, smiling, laughing and gesturing to me towards the back of his truck. He was offering me a ride.

"No thanks," I replied. He insisted and even told the other young man in the cab to get out and sit on the load in the cold, open truck. This was too good to refuse, so I relented, "Thank you. Thank you."

The young men lifted my bike onto the load. I got into the cab. It was warm and comfortable.

Even though he didn't understand any English, I explained, "What a break! You're the greatest! Just take me to the top of the Pass."

We talked and smiled and laughed all the way up the Pass. Neither of us knew what the other was saying but we understood each other perfectly.

We soon passed Keith and the truck finally left me at the top of Dry Valley Pass. I hugged the driver in gratitude. He laughed some more and helped me get my bike off the truck. The truck roared away taking my new, kind friend down the Pass to the south. The kindness of strangers...

The euphoria of the truck ride soon subsided. The top of the Pass was especially cold. A light snow began to fall. I tried to find a rock or a depression to shelter me from the wind but without success. About an hour and one-half later the van finally arrived with Keith. I was so grateful to see them that I forgot to be angry.

"I am beat. Let's camp," I said.

Keith complained, "We've gone less than 50 kilometers and we need to go further."

The driver through the translator said, "We'll stop at the Kumix Army Station at the bottom of the Pass."

The translator emphasized on his own, "It's too cold and windy. We can't camp on the Pass."

"How far to Kumix?" I asked.

"Just a few kilometers."

Before I had a chance to protest, Keith was on his bike, "It's too cold here. Let's go."

Off he flew down the first hill. All I could do was follow on my own bike. Even with the warm clothing I got from the van I felt as if I were freezing. In my weak condition even riding downhill further exhausted me. Once I got to the bottom of the Pass the Army Station was not there but the van had waited for me.

"How much further?," I asked.

"Twenty or thirty kilometers!"

Unable to go any further, I roared, "Get out! And put my bike on the truck." Sensing I was on the verge of hysteria, the driver without argument latched my bike atop the huge pile of baggage on the roof. Our overloaded van was even more dangerously overloaded but I didn't give a damn.

"Move over," I told the translator and I squeezed in the front seat. It was uncomfortable but warm. Keith was now far ahead. We passed an endless number of possible campsites but to no avail. I was too tired to object.

The Kumix Army Station was cold and crowded with PLA [People's Liberation Army] drivers and an army truck convoy. I was too tired to eat anything except one of my cans of chicken and some nuts. The cold grey weather matched my mood. Only my sleeping bag was user friendly. Drained and discouraged, I fell asleep.

8
FRIENDS OR FOES

More than anything I wanted to make this journey. I wanted it so much that I ignored a vital part of what makes any enterprise work - the people involved.

Slowly, I came to realize that I had repeated a possibly fatal error. In the past I had, in personal relationships, placed trust in people when I should not have. Now when my life may depend on it, I was aware that I knew nothing about my traveling companions.

The other thing I ignored was my own limitations. While still at home in San Francisco I had become so bogged down with pulling together the materials and supplies for this trip that I neglected what I needed most to work on - the condition of my body. Not only did I not work at building up my strength and stamina, I never rode my new bicycle the way I knew I had to. I didn't think I needed to work very hard to get myself in shape. Now when it was all for real, I had to deal with what I should have done months before. I knew that my ability to perform was questionable. It was my responsibility to deal with it I didn't. Now I was paying a heavy price.

As for responsibility, as leader of our group what exactly were Keith's responsibilities? Well, he obtained the permits form the Chinese government, which was no small feat. He determined what supplies we needed to bring along and he organized working with the possible sponsors. He put in a tremendous amount of preparatory effort and time to launch this expedition, to turn and idea into an adventure.

However, I couldn't help but question what other responsibilities or mental attitudes an "expedition" leader should have. There were basically just the two of us doing this. Yet Keith always referred to this trip in a very formal manner as "THE EXPEDITION." His obsession with that formality seemed weird to me. I never knew whether or not he had planned some huge expedition, with me being all that he was left with. I also didn't know what he was willing to sacrifice in order to complete the journey. Doing so meant something extraordinary for him - but I didn'now what.

When is an expedition leader a success? Is it the person that brings three members of the team to the top of a mountain and conquers it while three of the crew die in the attempt? Or is it the leader that fails to get there, but brings all the crew back alive? Keith knew I was 56 years old, and he knew I was very sick. I could have had anything from dysentery to cholera. Was it the act of a rational man to leave me up in the snow at Dry Valley Pass? Or was it simply immaturity and callousness?

What did I mean to Keith? I paid for my share of the trip and the supplies. There were basic costs that had to be met. The Chinese government required a support vehicle, a driver and a translator - that was whether there was 1 person, 2 people or 10 people. Keith might have had to pay out $15,000 or $18,000 in costs if he went alone. By paying my $10,000 share I reduced his costs considerably. Now that I had paid my money. had I become expendable?

I was also furious with Keith for bringing Amanda along. Not only was I not told about her before, I never knew if I paid for her to come along out of the money Keith got from me. It would have made it so much easier for me without her and her suitcases in the van. I could have ridden when I was tired which would have prevented the extreme exhaustion which led

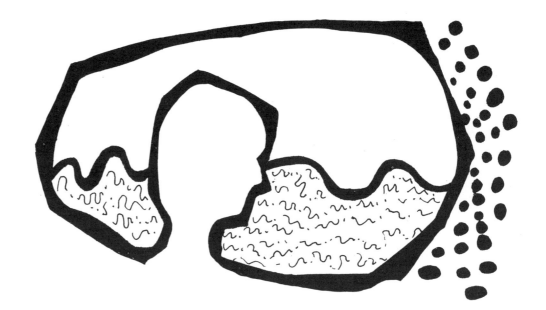

*Was it the act of a rational
man to leave me up in the snow
at Dry Valley Pass?*

to my being sick. A period of acclimatization could have been possible for me without her being there. While I was resentful at first, I did grow to like Amanda and was eventually extremely grateful for her presence. She was a good listener, and unlike Keith, she was compassionate and kind. She was a valuable resource since, as a Chinese, she knew what Tang and Chuan were really talking and thinking about.

To this day I have never made up my mind about Tang, the driver, and Chuan, the translator. Neither of them wanted to come on the trip. They were both extremely over-qualified if they were simply to be our escorts. I learned from Amanda that they were both made to "volunteer" for this duty by the China Mountaineering Association against their will.

Tang was from Beijing. He was a 37 year old former army driver who had become part of China's specialized group of mountain climbers. He had climbed many important peaks and served several historic expeditions in his 16 years with the China Mountaineering Association. He was a slight man, but very strong. Although he understood a little English, he spoke none. His wife was the first and only Chinese woman at that time to successfully ascend a peak over 20,000 feet. He was a worrier. He constantly complained that the truck was overloaded and the shock absorbers would snap. Amanda reported that he complained, "Nichols would collapse before the expedition made it to Kashgar," "the Kun Lun Mountains would be impossible to get through on bicycles," and "the Tibetan monsoons would drown the truck." This, of course, meant we should go no further, and should give up before these disasters struck.

Chuan, 28 years old, was from Urumchi. He had translated for several mountain climbing expeditions including an unsuccessful attempt in 1985 on K-2 by an American group. Chuan liked food, drinks, sleep, girls, and playing cards in that order. He played basketball and was surprisingly good at ping pong. He always had on dark glasses. The impression he gave was that of a friendly Asiatic Porky Pig. Chuan had a wife and daughter at home as well as many girlfriends who, he said, "liked him very much."

I calculated, allowing for nine hours of sleep, that they had at least ten hours of free time each day. They ate and drank whatever food or drinks the expedition had and supplemented that with local food and meals. All their expenses were paid. This life didn't seem to make Tang any heavier, but Chuan grew abeam weekly. Tang smoked and worried a lot and Chuan never worried about anything except the next meal. Neither got outwardly excited except about their card game.

They both complained to Keith that they had too much to do and didn't have enough sleep. The latter may have been true, since they stayed up until 2 or 3 a.m. each night. I never knew what they were doing, but they spent much of their time with the locals both in the villages and on the army bases. Their complaints to Keith worked because he agreed we would set up most of the camp, open our own cans of food, prepare our own food and be careful not to make them feel like "servants."

Their main task was to guide us through the country and make the arrangements where we were to stay or camp. They did that well with a few significant lapses. For example, Chuan mistranslated Tang's "two kilometers" into "twenty-five kilometers" at Tocsun, that cost us an extra fifteen kilometers of riding and the anxieties of being lost until Tang discovered Chuan's error. Another time I sat out in the blazing afternoon sun for two hours waiting because they forgot we were to meet at kilometer Post 1224. Again when Chuan was posted to show me where to turn off the road, he was asleep when I passed. I didn't see him asleep on the side of the road which led to the mishap that caused me to become lost at Post 930 on the road to Aksu. Chuan later explained, "A bus must have gone by so I couldn't see you."

Sitting in the van most of the day didn't seem to bother them. Except for eating and bathroom stops, neither got out. The vehicle had a heater, stereo and air conditioning. That may have been a good explanation for staying inside. In fact, when they gave me my food at noon, Chuan usually handed it out the window while I sat on the ground beside the road. The back seat was full and it would take up their space in the front if I sat inside. Later in the expedition I just moved them over and sat in the front seat with them. It was a welcome respite for me from the wind, the cold or the heat, depending on the lunch stop weather.

Although Tang and Chuan often behaved like cartoon characters, I wondered if they had a more sinister purpose. As we left we were told we weren't to photograph any bridges or army vehicles or facilities nor were we to have any contact with any local people without Tang. We were firmly told they had to be with us at all times. Were they sent along to spy on the army or on locals under the guise of being our escorts? Or were they to sabotage the journey? The Chinese don't like to say no, but to say yes and have us fail, well, that wouldn't be their fault. . .

9

GOODBYE, AMANDA

In the early days of our ride my need to survive overrode my ability to decipher intrigue. By the evening of the eighth day I was exhausted, and suffering uncontrolled diarrhea. I was also alternating between feeling the effects of heat stroke or shivering in the late afternoon drizzle. I did the best I could with the medicines I was carrying. Having no diagnostic expertise I really couldn't tell whether I was taking the right items or whether they were doing any good.

It was early evening when Tang met me in the van as I topped the last pass before Korla. I was coasting down into this headquarters city. The sight of the town suddenly revived me. From where I was I felt as if I were floating down from the a high desert hell into some holy city with streams, trees and greenness. To everyone's surprise and my own amazement, I'd made it to Korla in the allotted three days!

Following behind the van, I was very surprised when Tang turned into a large parking lot in front of a modern looking hotel. I was ecstatic with the thought of having hot water and clean sheets!

The two Mogul tents in the parking lot were reminders that this city was a headquarters for them in this region. Moguls were not a minority but the principal population in Korla. It was tempting to experience a night in their tents but they were dark and clammy. More importantly, they didn't have hot water.

The two Mogul tents in the parking lot were reminders that this city was a headquarters for them.

Streams from the Tian Shan had produced the oasis here in the Taklamaton Desert, and a huge, salt water lake to the east, Bagrax Hu. The surrounding land produces fruit, vegetables, greens, diary produce and fish that are shipped throughout China.

As I looked out our hotel windows after a bath and a pre-dinner nap, the pleasure of being comfortable and clean made me doubt my own desperate memories of the last few days. Only a day before I had labored under the sun up Elm Tree pass into the desolation of the Gobi. There was no life there, only the rush of a truck passing now and then, and two wild camels. The camels watched me with great interest until I pedaled close to them. Then they loped away. There were no trees to be seen on Elm Tree pass, let alone an elm tree. As an indication of how rare plant life was here, a sign by the highway on this desolate mountain pass listed the distance on a side road to the "elm tree."

The pass should have been called "cotton candy" pass because of the fluffy, white asbestos that was being mined by the Chinese along the road. The miners lived in primitive hovels made of grass mats in these isolated camps. I was sure they were prisoners who needed no guards since there was nowhere to escape to. Actually, they were volunteers who received extra pay for the hard work in these rugged and remote mountains. Since our Korla hotel was for officials and executives, these miners never were treated to the luxuries that I enjoyed.

I was too ill to do any sightseeing around Korla, so I decided to rest all day on our day off. That proved an illusory objective since practically the whole day was spent in arguments, complaints and counter-complaints. By the time we reached Korla I knew my survival depended on some concessions by "the Expedition."

"You have to slow down. I can't go so far each day. I'm still sick!" I argued. I also told Keith, "We're supposed to pick the stopping places."

It had been understood earlier that we would avoid staying in villages and army camps wherever possible. I was sure camping out was safer, cleaner, and easier than sleeping and eating in army camps or native villages. These places were usually filthy and infested with vermin. I had even said so in my earliest letters. Tang, Chuan, and Keith listened but said nothing.

Tang, through Chuan, demanded a second van or truck, and everyone seemed to think that I should pay for it so that I could ride in it. Keith complained that we were going too slowly and that I was holding them back. I wanted time to get well and strong. Keith wanted me to stop riding and get another truck to carry me and the bicycle. Tang was sure I wouldn't make it anyway and wanted an extra van so that there would be room for me and extra baggage.

These issues, already a sore point, became a constant plague on the expedition. We met several times at Korla, and got so far as to meet with a proposed driver for a second vehicle. He was a friend of Tang's and anxious to join us. Tang, speaking through Chuan, and sometimes Amanda, spent hours in our room discussing the problem. We were often not sure whether the ideas were Tang's or Chuan's. But at least those two were in apparent agreement.

"The van is overloaded. We can't even make it to Kashgar," Tang repeated.

"Why? We've made it so far, over Dry Valley Pass and Elm Tree Pass," Keith replied.

"The shocks will break at the slightest bump, so we have to go too slowly."

"You don't have far to go each day, so drive slowly," I interrupted (since the discussion was mainly between Tang and Keith).

"I can't be responsible if the vehicle is damaged and there is no way to fix it."

Again I entered the conversation, "We'll take the risk."

Keith added, "Can you lighten the load?"

"No, but to go on you must throw away half of the things you now have on the van. We'll need to load more food and water at Kashgar for the journey through the mountains."

"If we drop some of our supplies, extra bike equipment, camera gear and clothing, what can you get along without?" Keith asked.

"Nothing. We only have a minimal amount of stuff anyway. The rest is needed for the journey," Chuan replied without even translating Keith's question to Tang.

We all agreed it would be good to lighten the load but we disagreed as to whose things should be left behind. As the conversation continued, it became evident that they were looking at me. I soon caught the drift.

"No!" I said adamantly. "I can't part with my vitamins and food supplements (a suitcase full) or extra food (four boxes). Otherwise I'll never make it."

I said it harshly enough to discourage, temporarily, their pursuing me on this subject, and no one else wanted to part with anything.

We finally agreed we needed another vehicle but deadlocked again.

"You say the van can't proceed. Since CMA agreed to provide the transportation for the expedition, you must get another vehicle at CMA expense," I argued. Tang disagreed, "No. You brought too much stuff so you'll have to pay."

Relenting, Keith asked, "How much would another vehicle cost?"

Tang replied, "We can get a van for 2,000 or a truck for 3,000 US."

"That's outrageous, but it's okay so long as CMA pays for it," I countered.

Chuan again replied without consulting Tang, "That's not possible."

The negotiations stalled on that note, but complaints about the overloaded van and my inadequacies were to continue daily. In the meantime, we decided to press forward from Korla to Asku and risk a breakdown, either mine or the van's.

Amanda tried to stay uninvolved in these conversations. However, she spoke Chinese and English and was an excellent translator. She also understood the innuendos and complexities of everyone's position, being familiar with Chinese thinking in general and a friend of Keith's.

More importantly, she liked everyone and had no personal stake in any of the issues. She was slowly becoming a mediator. Often, she would sit unobtrusively during these discussions, or quietly listen while riding in the van, and tell us later what Tang and Chuan were saying to each other. That proved to be helpful, but didn't lead to anyone's changing positions.

I had initially resented Amanda's presence in an already overcrowded van, but as the days passed I began to wish she would stay the whole journey. However, she had already decided to leave us at Korla. I didn't blame her.

On our last night at the hotel I asked if we could talk alone. Keith overheard me and seemed a little surprised but said nothing.

"Sure, maybe later," she said a little hesitantly. "I'll let you know when I finish packing and getting ready."

I was afraid she was avoiding me, so about 9:00 that night I went to her room when she was alone. Amanda was an intelligent woman in her thirties. She was single, pleasant and had a good sense of humor. At the same time, she was tough, as a business woman had to be in China. She worked for the same company as Keith and spent most of her time in China at Tienjin, or in Hong Kong. Although she and Keith were long time friends and business associates, I was unsure of their personal relationship.

A little timid about how to get the discussion going, we dealt with generalities for a while. In the course of the conversation, she told me her sister was a famous movie actress and that she had been involved in producing movies in Hong Kong. She impressed me as being well able to take care of herself.

I asked her about an incident that had happened a few days earlier, "The only army camp I liked was Milan, where we were refused entry. If there really was no room for us, why did they keep us waiting outside the gate for two hours?"

"That's because they were radioing army headquarters in Urumchi and Beijing about what to do with us. We had all the permits but they couldn't believe we were allowed into such militarily sensitive areas."

"Why did they finally bring us in for tea?"

"To tell you more politely to go away."

"What were the real reasons?"

"No one is supposed to know," she said.

"Tell me."

"Didn't you notice all the soldiers were unusually well dressed and that there were a lot of officers and higher ranking personnel, some even with families, or that the buildings seemed much better and newer."

"Yes, I noticed all that, but what did that mean?"

"Milan is a nuclear research facility for the army and is involved with weapons testing."

I was surprised but remembered that China does do its nuclear testing in the Taklamaton Desert further to the south and east. "No wonder they didn't want two Americans wandering around inside the base with strange bicycles and a Chinese speaking femme fatale. We might have stolen earth shaking secrets." We laughed.

"No sensible self-respecting spy would be around here, let alone bicycle through all of this," she added.

"Amanda, can you help explain what's going on?"

"Sure."

"I'm not feeling well, everyone says I can't make it, but I don't want to quit. Is Keith trying to ride me into the ground so I'll stop and go home?"

"I don't know. Keith is very serious about succeeding. This is his first expedition. He's always more interested in his goals than anything else. It's what his life is all about now."

"Will he run over me?"

"I don't think so. But I can't give you any guarantees. He wants you to get through. It's important to him. But he doesn't think you can make it and would rather have you ride in the van. He's not an empathetic person. But I've worked with him a long time and he's a good friend."

"What do Tang and Chuan want?"

"To go home. They don't think the expedition can succeed. Tang really fears for your safety and feels responsible for it. He thinks you will collapse before you get to Kashgar and says there is no chance that you could make it over the mountains, and he's been there before."

"Can I trust him?"

"Maybe, but you must be strong in demanding what you want."

"Do they feel the trip is beneath their abilities?"

"Tang has been in charge and part of many mountain expeditions in China. Chuan is ambitious and wants to be a translator with the foreign service or with foreign business, not a tour guide."

Time had run out. Amanda had to finish packing and I had to get my bike ready for the next part of our journey.

"I feel better just talking to you, Amanda."

"Thank you. I really hope it works out."

"At first I resented your using up space in the van, but now I'm sorry you're leaving."

"Me too. But this is my last chance to leave until Kashgar and that's over 600 miles away. The atmosphere is a little too charged for me. I'm supposed to be on a vacation, and even my one cubic foot in the back seat under all the camping gear takes up too much space."

"Yes, you might be the subject of the next negotiations and be dumped along with my food boxes in the desert," I replied.

We laughed and hugged each other. I didn't go to the airport to see her off the next day. But from the hotel window I saw her plane turn north over the mountains towards Urumchi. Suddenly I felt alone, I knew I had lost my only ally. I've not seen her since she left that day.

*From the hotel window I saw
her plane turn north over
the mountains towards Urumchi.*

10 ENDLESS HORIZONS

I left Korla around 9:00 in the morning. Keith left two hours later because of a problem with his free-wheel. Tang, still concerned about the overload, was readjusting the boxes on top of the van as I left. Rested, full of a large breakfast, clean and re-inspired, I rode through the town and onto the main highway west towards Kashgar. It was overcast and cool with only a slight breeze.

The terrain immediately out of town was much as it would be for the next few days. We were cycling along the northern edge of the Taklamaton Desert in the Gobi. Tian Shan, the "heavenly mountains," were usually on our right to the north. Sometimes they were only barren rock foothills close by, at other times imposing white-capped ranges, loomed far away. To our left were the endless wastes of the Gobi.

More often than not the views were obscured near and far by overcast skies, heat waves and sometimes straggly mists in the morning or haze in the afternoon. The lower mountains, comprised of pyrites, sandstone, granite and volcanic rock were varying shades of black, grey, red, brown, and yellow. The foothills often became standing rainbows.

In the lights of dawn and dusk the desert to the south seemingly stretched beyond our sight forever. As the ancients traveled this route the terrain undoubtedly confirmed their beliefs that the earth ended somewhere. What more likely place than this vast, rocky, dead plateau?

The overall impression was that the road never ended. As the paved road followed the old central Silk Route, history seemed enshrouded in the limitless horizons. I would cycle as far as I could see the road in front of me, and when I got there the road ahead was just as it was before. There was no awareness of distance traveled. I could have been on a stationary bicycle on which the timer had been set for ten hours.

Every twenty or thirty kilometers, a stream or small river would transform a patch of the Gobi into different worlds - oases of small villages - houses, irrigated fields, and pasture land. The suddenness of the vegetation, trees, and water were pleasant shocks each time. On seeing me bicycle, the local people seemed amazed. I smiled at them as I rode but usually didn't stop. Whenever I did, a crowd would materialize.

Once, when we camped in a pasture near a few houses, too small to even be considered a village, it was extraordinary how quickly scores of people suddenly appeared to gawk at us in our camp, watching our every move. Outdoor toiletry and modesty became impossible. I settled for informal exhibitionism - the observers only smiled and watched.

In spite of assurances at Korla that the winds blew from east to west and were stronger in the morning, they actually blew against us from west to east and got stronger as the day wore on.

Except for the Moguls at Korla and the large number of new immigrants in the towns from central China, the natives along our way were mostly Uygurs. They were an indigenous minority, friendly, colorful, and comfortable in their own culture, resentful at the influx of Chinese. It was Sunday and bazaar day, at a village called Luntai, as I bicycled past. The road was crowded with horses, carts, bicycles and pedestrians. All of them were going to town, obviously in their best, most colorful clothes, with smiles of anticipation. They shared their enthusiasm as I rode past, friendly and curious about the foreigner riding an exotic bicycle. It would have been fun to spend time there but as usual I had to keep going. A visit to Luntai would also have created a mob scene.

One afternoon Tang stopped at a primary school in a village, Yeyungou. We stayed in the headmaster's small office that had four bench-bed combinations. The floor was filthy concrete. Flies swarmed over everything and seemed to be thicker inside than outside. Both villagers and school staff crowded into our room to stare at us, talking and joking with themselves, occasionally spitting on the floor, but generally being very agreeable.

School was in session when we arrived, so I volunteered, through Chuan, to teach. That resulted in a meeting, after which they led me to the headmaster's quarters (a single dark room in a small adobe complex, with a small, hibachi-type stove), where the principal and his wife and at least two children lived. The walls and dirt floor were heavily covered with Persian-type rugs.

After a while, a few teachers and some other people brought in two shy little girls. Obviously picked as an example, they were about 9 years old. The headmaster told them to learn from me and told me to "go ahead and teach," while a room full of adults stared at us. I was embarrassed about what to do and didn't know whether to sing, talk about America, do arithmetic, or stand on my head. The two victims were more troubled and almost on the verge of tears at all the attention. They blushed and couldn't even speak in answer to my asking their names. I tried singing a song, but they only looked more pained. I became more uncomfortable and tried to figure out how I could resign as a teacher.

"Have the children ever seen an American before?" I asked the principal through the translator.

"Yes," he replied, "Japanese came to the village last year."

Trying to rescue the situation, I told the principal, "This is a little hard on these two students. Let's try something with the whole class."

The principal then called another meeting of teachers and staff. After some discussion, they decided to let me try again, probably knowing I couldn't do worse than I had with these first two students. I was escorted to a square room about 24 feet wide with at least fifty children inside. They sat on benches four at a desk. The desks reminded me of historical pictures of schools in California in the 1880's. I proceeded to try to teach the whole class how to sing *Row, Row, Row Your Boat*. They warmed to the task immediately and caught on quickly. Soon we were all laughing. While they could sing together, learning the song by rote, I was unable to get them to sing in rounds. They were still giggling when I left.

The most striking thing about the class was how similar they looked to children in my hometown. Some looked Mogul, a few Asian but most looked Caucasian. Their skin color varied from white to brown and their eyes, while mostly brown, were sometimes blue and even gray. Perhaps their eclectic appearance reflected the village's location on the Silk Route. For centuries the local villagers had been adding to their population all types of exotic strangers - perhaps even the remnants of Alexander's Greek army, Persians, Indians or Europeans.

That evening I ate from my own food cans while the others ate at a thatched roadside stand. They complained about having to eat under filthy conditions and suffered intestinally afterwards. I felt it was a small revenge for their not camping out on the open desert, where at least the dirt and sand was clean. I wanted to say, "I told you so," but refrained.

A couple of nights later when we were forced to camp out, because no villages or camps were near, Chuan, Tang, and Keith held a conference. They thought I was asleep but I overhead most of the conversation.

Tang and Chuan kept saying, "The van is overloaded and we can't go on."

Keith promised, "We'll jettison more stuff, especially Alan's four food boxes."

They all had their own versions of why and how, "Alan will never make it." Or even if by some freak chance I made it to Kashgar, "he would never get through the mountains beyond."

While it might not have been impressive to the three of them, I was proud of what I had accomplished thus far. Their talk only increased my determination. Besides, whatever it was that made me so sick was finally starting to disappear. I could feel I was getting stronger and stronger.

11 AKSU

It was at this point in the journey that the unfortunate ride which took us to Aksu covered in Chapter 1 took place. To celebrate finding each other again we decided to reward ourselves with a morning of rest.

By habit, I now woke early. The rays of the early morning sun filtering through the trees into the gardens of our hotel created a lovely aura of serenity. They lit up the snow-capped Massif, Tomur Feng, close by on the Russian border over 7,000 meters high. It was a cool, clear day. Feeling better and stronger, I was convinced Kashgar was within my range.

I took a two hour stroll around Aksu, a bustling, busy city full of shops and people. Everybody seemed to be on the move or selling something. The center of the city was typical of the smaller towns in the outlying regions of China. It hummed with movement, with new construction, with change, with dust, with industrialization, and growth.

The center of the "downtown" was a police box for directing traffic at the intersection of four unpaved dusty boulevards. The larger buildings located along the boulevards included offices and stores. The department store, a few small food stores and the miscellaneous shops were drab and uninteresting. The people were unusually diverse and extraordinary. The women fascinated me. Some were dressed in traditional heavy brown or black clothes with veils over their faces, while others rode bicycles in short skirts.

After lunch and an interview with a local newspaper, we prepared to leave the hotel compound. We were told that the expedition had been the subject of several print articles and TV coverage throughout China, "another first in American-Chinese friendship," they said. We all smiled. Amazing what feelings can be hidden behind the mask of a smile.

During the good-byes, I noticed that the local newspaper photographer had the latest and best Nikon equipment. I knew that there was no way locally to even process color pictures and was surprised that they used such sophisticated and expensive equipment. How did Nikon find its way to this small town in the Taklamaton Desert, hundreds of miles from anywhere in this remote corner of the earth? I was informed that Nikon had given the equipment to the newspaper and that hundreds of other small town newspapers in China had received similar gifts. I had to hand it to the Japanese for being extremely clever about setting up how to move into a future market. There was a lesson to be learned.

In the days that followed, I further refined my early morning starts by preparing everything I needed for the next day's ride the night before. That way I could get up and leave camp as soon as the pre-dawn light allowed. On a relatively flat paved road, I could average 25 kilometers an hour in the morning before the winds came up, and then after lunch struggle for another 40 kilometers in the afternoon against the wind.

Keith kept extending our distance goals so I always seemed to be struggling to make camp at the end of the day. He also became more and more anxious about our slow progress. He was consumed by thoughts of whether we could make it over the mountains, or through Tibet. I knew we were behind schedule and was upset with myself, but Keith was a man possessed.

With the increased pressures and the need to ride longer each day, my buttocks became raw. I developed painful saddle sores that could only be relieved by pumping the bicycle standing up on the pedals. It would work for a while, then my legs ached more than my rear. At that point I would sit until the discomfort reversed itself.

Up to the time we had reached Aksu, I had been too exhausted to absorb much of anything. My goal then was just to survive. By this part of our trip, other thoughts became more important. I was alone cycling all day, neither comfortable with nor enjoying my companions. My diary reported one day's camp where we finished early and the others left to eat in a truck stop a few miles back down the road:

> *"I sit alone before my tent. The rest have gone to a village lunch stop to eat. I am sad that I am here. The appeal of things is an illusion for the ignorant like me. Joy is in people more than in solitude."*

I knew I was getting physically stronger, but I was also becoming depressed. All this, with the stress of the journey, came to a head one evening after a long day of cycling. I pedaled up over a small rise and saw the camp. To my relief, the day's ride was over. I rode into camp, laid my bike down and myself beside it on the desert floor to rest. Usually I would do this about half an hour until my energies resurged. Only then was I ready to put my gear together for the night and start thinking of a snack, dinner, etc. This particular time Keith walked up to me and sat down on a rock. I tensed, sure of another confrontation about the usual subjects.

"I am going to take a little walk up the mountain but we have to talk," he told me. "We [he meant me] are going to have to help more with the camp. Chuan and Tang have complained."

"But they have virtually nothing to do, so why have you agreed that we have to do more and they less?" I asked.

"Well, to be honest, the main thing is that you are not doing your share because you're so exhausted from each day's ride."

I blew up, "You're driving me into the ground and you know it! An expedition leader is supposed to see to the welfare of the group. By paying attention only to yourself and by trying to get rid of me, you've just demonstrated that your not fit to lead anything - now or ever!"

That was the start of a long, heated argument. The outcome was we would agree in advance to the number of kilometers to travel each day for the remainder of the trip, and that the distances would not be increased without both of us consenting. If I couldn't make it, I agreed that I would quit or get another van and ride in it. On the other hand, if we got ahead of schedule, we would have more rest days or slow down. Keith agreed to prepare a proposed itinerary for each day's travel for review and discussion in Kashgar.

On May 29th we made our greatest mileage to date, 153 kilometers. The weather was perfect. Since we were heading south, the afternoon crosswinds actually had a tailwind effect. The road was well paved, with a slight roll. To my right, most of the way was a beautiful range of red, grey and white rock cliffs. The erosion pattern made it appear like a large, multicolored accordion. On the other side of those cliffs, a few miles away was the Russian border.

For a few kilometers we passed several small lakes. Each one was bordered with brilliant white salt. Often there were dunes of salt. The alkaline waters were a deep blue. A green moss also grew at the edge of the waters, adding another color to the scene. The whole area was a fairyland of beauty under a sparkling sun. In order to have lunch and take a swim, I decided to stop and walk over to one of the lakes close to the highway. But this beauty was better enjoyed at a distance. The shores were bogs of mud and each pond was guarded by swarms of gnats. I lost the temptation to dawdle and moved on.

At the higher points on the highway, where the trucks were going slower, roadside vendors opened "truck stops." Usually, these stops consisted of a man sitting under a mat held up by four posts. He would have a pile of brush firewood, or two twenty gallon oil drums, or a small stock of food with warm sugar water or beer for sale. With precious little vegetation left, even the small firewood trade was turning the area into a wasteland.

Every now and then a dog would rush at me, barking and snarling. My speed always increased with the sudden flow of adrenaline. Frightened, I peddled as fast as I could to get away. I grew to hate those damn dogs. We were so far away from anywhere that I'm sure most of these dogs had never seen a bicycle. It was big and it was moving fairly fast, so what do they do? Attack. They gave me a hell of a time. It was enough to turn the most ardent animal lover into a butcher.

Once, when the afternoon winds were especially strong, I tried again to catch a ride on a passing truck. It had slowed down coming up a rolling hill. I grabbed the tailgate chain. Immediately after I caught hold, the truck began to speed up and swerved from side to side. It was as if I was at the end of a crack-the-whip at 40 miles an hour. I let go as soon as I could get my bicycle under control again and concluded that my original impressions on Dry Valley Pass against hitchhiking were correct.

Every now and then a dog would rush at me barking and snarling. I grew to hate those damn dogs.

May 30th became a historic day for me at the time although we rode "only" 140 kilometers. As my diary recited:

> *"May 30, 140 kilometers. Slight to moderate head-winds, also crosswinds, hot, overcast. 7:45 a.m. to 3:35 p.m. This was the first day that (cyclist) Keith admits he was tired from the day's ride."*

Ah - the satisfaction of sarcasm. A few days ago they were having stomach problems because of the stuff they ate, now Keith was tired! I didn't want unpleasant things to happen to anyone else, but since they refused to acknowledge that I wasn't sick and slow on purpose, maybe feeling a bit of what I felt would foster some kindness and compassion. Here entered a glimmer of hope.

With Kashgar only 155 kilometers away, I knew I would make it! The thought of being in this ancient city was exciting. Weeks ago Kashgar had been only a whisper in my imagination. As we came closer, the ancient city seemed to draw me to it. The last day I was positively buoyant, singing to myself and pumping faster with each hour. At last to be at the hub of the ancient Silk Route at the crossroads of Central Asia!

The thought of our two planned rest days in Kashgar was pure joy! The journey so far had been, as I now laughingly reminded myself, no vacation.

12 THE DAILY GRIND

Keith considered it imperative that the "THE EXPEDITION" move faster. He often reminded me that our daily mileage was only about half what he could do. In his mind it was obvious I was delaying the expedition. It was difficult to put up with his continual annoyance with me. The trip was painful enough without someone constantly telling me what a screw-up I was.

China does not follow the concept of different time zones. All China is on Beijing time. We were about the same distance from Beijing as San Francisco is from Chicago. When it is 7 a.m. in Chicago it is 5 a.m. in San Francisco. So if we seemed to be getting off very late each morning, it was an illusion. While it may be 7 a.m. according to our clock set to Beijing time, it was actually the crack of dawn where we were.

Besides the eight hours I usually slept at night, my cycling days followed somewhat of a pattern. Often I would wake up with a jolt fearing that it was late. It was dark but some stars would have been obliterated by the first light from the eastern sky. I always hurried to get ready to ride, to be on the road by the first light, around 8:00 a.m.

If I left long before Keith woke up, I avoided his criticism. Also I could complete most of the days run before the afternoon heat and winds slowed me down. Since he cycled faster, he usually passed me. After a while it became a game for me to see how long during the day I could lead.

7:00 - 8:15 a.m. I had "breakfast in bed" from my own food box - dried fruit, nuts, part of a Pemmican bar, Chinese packaged cookies and a huge assortment of vitamins, minerals and food supplements, each in a separate capsule suggested by Dr. Rudy. They consisted of: two multivitamins, one riboflavin, one calcium/magnesium, one garlic, one EPA 1000 fish oil, one lipotropic factors, one bromanase, and, at high altitudes, one octocosonal. Except for the riboflavin, I took the same capsules at noon and at night. My stomach didn't complain at first, but after a while all that stuff did upset it and I cut down on the prescription. After my "supplemented breakfast," I rolled up my sleeping bag and one-man mountain tent, packed my gear and put it in the van.

8:00 - 10:30 a.m. I rode with determination. On a good paved road I could ride 56 to 64 kilometers in this period. On unpaved, rocky, up and down (mostly up) mountain roads, I could usually cover about one-third that distance. I drank from my water bottles and sometimes ate a little while riding.

10:30 a.m. I was ready for a short rest stop, some water, a bite of a Pemmican bar, a few nuts and some dried fruit plus five more Dr. Rudy specials.

10:30 - 11:45 a.m. or so. Under good conditions on a paved road I could ride another 24 kilometers.

12 noon (approximately). For lunch I ate another Pemmican bar, nuts, dried fruit and sometimes a small can of chicken or tuna fish, usually supplemented from the truck with some canned fruit, cookies or bread and sometimes warm Chinese beer or fruit juice, all with

the usual Dr. Rudy supplements. At the noon break, I liked to rest or nap 20 minutes and take a few pictures. The camera was too heavy to carry on my bike so I left it in the van. When it all had to be moved by pedal power, every ounce counted.

1:00 - 3:00/5:00 p.m. (The exact time to end the day's ride depended on how far I had to go.) After lunch, I became weaker, the winds were stronger and the weather usually deteriorated.

The farthest I rode in a single day was 135 miles. The shortest distance we rode on paved roads was 30 miles. We knew that on the mountain roads, we would be doing well to ride 20 miles in a day. We expected the worst roads and conditions would be in the Kun Lun Mountains and Western Tibet.

4:30 - 5:00 p.m. This was a time for recovery from the day's effort with rest, whatever liquid was available and a third round of Dr. Rudy's lipex/carnetine supplements. I was always tired and had to lie down on the ground for a while. My buttocks were often so tender I couldn't sit.

5:00 - 6:00 p.m. Chore time - to set up the tents, roll out the sleeping bag, fill the water bottles, clean and repair the bike and prepare for the next morning. Usually the winds were at their worst at this time of day so that keeping the tents from blowing down or away was often difficult.

6:00 - 8:00 p.m. It took about two hours each day to prepare and eat dinner. Tang and Chuan sometimes made dinner for everyone - canned fish or pork, eggs, noodles or rice and often canned or sometimes locally acquired fresh vegetables, greens like garlic or onion. To avoid stomach problems I tried to be careful about what I ate and supplemented the meal with the Dr. Rudy specials plus some of the dried or canned foods I brought with me.

8:00 - 9:00 p.m. After dinner we usually chatted about the next days ride, sometimes I played Chinese Fourteens, a card game, with Tang and Chuan.

9:00 - 11:00 p.m. Because all China operated on Beijing, time sunset wasn't until about 10:30 p.m. During the evenings I usually read, wrote or did nothing. Often I would wander off from camp and take pictures of the area. For half an hour before bed I listened to one of my five tapes of classical music. Many nights I dozed off listening to music, gazing at star-filled skies. On other nights the music dissolved the pains, the dirt, the storms or anxieties about the next days ride.

11:00 p.m. I was asleep by 11:00, often on the ground in my sleeping bag, sometimes curled-up pretzel-like on the four foot van seat and, too often, on a hard dirty cot in a mud hut or an army camp.

In retrospect, most of what I did was eat, sleep, drink and pedal. That took no mental effort so my mind was mostly blank during the long pedaling hours. There might have been some mystical benefits but no revelations resulted from such non-thought. The long days, however, reinforced my determination to keep going.   I especially wanted to return to the holy mountain, Kailas, hundreds of miles away in Tibet. I knew that when I finally got home, all the pain would stop and the hard-earned residue of joyful memory would last the rest of my life.

To force myself to concentrate on the journey, I purposely brought nothing to read except a book about the Tibetan saint, Milarepa. The themes of his own life and his teachings were meditation, asceticism and solitude. His life and ideas were beyond my understanding. He meditated for two years in a cave eating only nettles. The lack of food reportedly transformed him into a living ghost and the nettles turned him green.

Dr. Rudy's capsules didn't turn me green, but this ride was surely an ascetic experience. Maybe in a larger sense the journey was a meditation. I sometimes felt in spite of all the

exercise I was really doing nothing - maybe that feeling arose because mental activity was and is such a part of my normal life.

To keep my mind alive, I contemplated, meditated, self-analyzed and daydreamed. I also visualized friends and family. Strangely, such diversions didn't last long, although I had hours every day to indulge them. I tried contemplating an important idea for a whole day - love, gratitude, solitude, beauty, peace, time, joy, anger or generosity. But looking back over the day, I often discovered very little time was actually spent on the planned focus.

I made some personal resolutions; for example, I vowed never to take anyone on a hike or bike ride that was beyond their physically comfortable limits. As I rode, my attention turned to sights along the road, but they seemed too melt quickly from my mind. Now, as I think back, those scenes are permanently etched into my memory.

Once on the road, I counted kilometers. Along the paved roads a numbered post or painted

Once on the road I counted kilometers.
I often became obsessed with numbers.
It was like a chant...

numbers on the pavement marked every kilometer from Urumchi to Kashgar. Using these markers and my watch, I made endless calculations. (I calculated I had to pedal 1,560,000 full revolutions to complete the journey.) How fast was I going? How many kilometers to go that day or to the next town? How many kilometers did I ride in the last hour? How many miles was that? I often became obsessed with numbers, kilometer objectives, mini-objectives, speed, etc. It was like a chant.

Mystics know that chants and repetitive rituals hold your immediate attention so the rest of your mental processes can become blank. Once the mind is blank, the way is said to be open to experience the higher faculty of human consciousness, the worlds of spirit. But for me the kilometer focus became so compulsive that any possible spiritual aspect of this journey was ignored. It became so compulsive that I finally stopped by forcing myself to turn my eyes away whenever I passed a marker.

What struck me most about my first month of riding was the amount of time my mind was blank. I wondered, is this journey the road to nirvana or nothingness? Were they the same? Or was I actually dead and this was some type of test before I was sent to heaven or hell? Was I simply going down the long bright tunnel people report in near death experiences, would I meet St. Peter, or would I meet the ancient Egyptian god who would test me by seeing if my heart was lighter than a feather? At some point along the journey, any of these seemed possible.

Imagining how others might analyze me at home, my final psychoanalytic self-diagnosis was, "I was out to lunch."

When I got to the top of the pass,
I saw the fabled Kashgar...

13 KASHGAR TRIUMPH

The world was made up of depressing shades of gray - a light gray sky, a dark gray desert bordered by the even darker gray mountains on the horizon. This was in stark contrast to my jubilation. Only 75 kilometers to Kashgar. Kashgar - my triumph! After all of the misery, the pain and the anger - I was going to make it to Kashgar!

I rose especially early and cycled quickly along the road, well ahead of Keith and the van. This was my special day and I didn't want them to intrude on my joy. Several hours later it began to sprinkle as I approached a tree-lined highway. "This must be Kashgar," I thought, a little disappointed at the dry, colorless sparsely populated roadside. But the road then turned left away from the valley and into foothills. I bicycled alongside a wide rocky riverbed and then up a small pass.

When I got to the top of the pass, I saw, a few miles away, the fabled Kashgar. This was the promised city. The lush, fertile emerald green valley lay below me surrounded by the desolate deserts and mountains beyond. Kashgar seemed a paradise, a respite from the dangers, the stresses, the monotony of the road through Central Asia. I then thought that for at least three thousand years, travelers coming over this pass must have experienced the same elation, "We're here!"

I coasted the three miles down into the green valley. The rain had settled the dust. The gardens, fields, and the flowers along the roads sparkled with raindrops. Keith caught up with me and we cycled into the city together. Chuan and Tang were unsure where our hotel was so we followed them as they meandered around the town. Compared with the isolation of the last few weeks, Kashgar was a shock. Crowds were everywhere. We were suddenly immersed in people. They all seemed to be going somewhere - on bicycles, buses, carts, tractors, wagons, camels and horses. The streets overflowed with animals and people of all shapes, sizes, and colors.

For centuries Kashgar was the capital of a kingdom once known as Shu Le. The city with two thousand years of recorded history seemed to live up to its reputation as the true center of Central Asia. For thousands of years caravans linked it with the Kirghiz pastures and Mogul hordes to the north, India and Tibet to the south, Europe and the Middle East over the Yanguan and Yumen passes to the west and around the dreaded Taklamaton Gobi to China and the east.

Like the countless numbers before me I was elated to be at this refuge for the traveler from the bleakness of the surrounding countryside. My only worry was that our lodgings would be just as ancient and worn out by dirt and hard use as the central city.

The van finally turned back outside the central city to a wooded area and then into a large separate compound. I laughed aloud at the sight. I couldn't believe our hotel was modern and obviously newly completed. It was set in flowered gardens. I was overjoyed, we would spend two days here.

The dank gray bathroom, and the premature disintegration of the paint, carpet, and furniture in my room did nothing to dampen my enthusiasm. The clean sheets and towels, running water (even warm water - hot water from a tap had long ceased to be a reality), mattressed beds with clean pillows and pillowcases, clean floors, edible meals and a new thermos of boiled drinking water seemed to me the quintessence of civilization.

As soon as I entered my sunlit room, I undressed to take a bath. The lukewarm brownish water left me much cleaner, relaxed and very tired. The clean sheets on my bed were a luxurious temptation I couldn't resist.

After an hours nap, I awoke and immediately wanted to see Kashgar. Keith was asleep in his room, but I found Tang and Chuan in theirs. In answer to my request that they drive me back into town, they told me they had "things they had to do with the van." My suspicions were later confirmed that their plans with the van were more ephemeral than real. When I went back to their room to tell them I was going to walk to town, they too were asleep.

About a half mile from the hotel compound, I found several unpaved roads leading towards town. As I got closer, the townspeople and farmers all seemed to be flowing in the same direction. It reminded me of a crowd going to a sporting event or a fair, with everyone old and young, well-dressed and shabbily dressed, talkative, carrying bundles, excited. They were all going towards the flood basin below the city. I followed.

Less than a mile from the river, noises of crowds and animals floated up from the direction we all seemed to be heading. A small river meandered through a flood basin. As I came through some scrub bushes and small trees. There was a row of mud huts and buildings, just beyond I picked up a wide dirt path. Suddenly I was at the fair - a combined farmer's market, garage sale, and flea market on a huge scale. Thousands of farmers, herders, city

*a man could risk everything
for those eyes...*

dwellers, and others were either buying or selling something - camels, horses, pigs, goats, sheep, hides, leather goods, weapons, knives, garden vegetables, cooked foods, lumber, saddles, furniture, clothing, shoes. With a few exceptions, most of the products and certainly the way of doing business, were at least 2000 years old. Everyone was negotiating, shouting, greeting others, arguing, and laughing. No one paid much attention to me, unless I happened to be standing next to them, in which case, they gave me a startled look and went back to whatever they were doing.

The market roared with noise and life. Being used to having crowds form around me, I was surprised that I could be so anonymous. I didn't remember that the people of Kashgar and their ancestors, the keepers of the Silk Route, had already experienced centuries of exotic travelers on their way to India, Tibet, China, Mongolia, Samarkand and Xinjiang. Compared to all of them, I guess I wasn't all that interesting.

I was unimpressed with the cattle, but the small, spirited horses were marvelous. A dashing red turbaned, young horse trader with a broad smile and flashing eyes, spurred his horses up and down between the rows of horses for sale. He knew how to show off their spirit to appreciative onlookers and buyers. In contrast to the nervous horses, the camels in the adjoining area calmly watched, obviously disdainful of such wild demonstrations of wasted energy.

Most of the women at the market wore veils and heavy dark clothing. Only their eyes gave a hint of what they really looked like. Sometimes their dark eyes would turn to me. Because I had been alone so long in the desert, my imagination conjured visions of the women of the Arabian Nights. A few caught me watching them. Our eyes would lock for a moment, I was fascinated. In our modern society in which men and women constantly interact, the stories in operas, fairy tales and old novels in which one becomes mesmerized by someone at a glance seems silly. But here a man could risk everything for those eyes. I could now better understand the source of men oppressing women - because of their power. And the power of women here was especially evident. They could easily become an obsession. To be close to a woman, to touch one, to have one. When it is not possible, the thoughts of them were consuming.

That night was the best sleep I'd had in weeks. The next day we took the van to the Id Kah Mosque in the center of town. The four hundred year old Mosque, once an important seminary of learning for Muslim leaders, was dilapidated. The paint on the buildings had long since peeled off and the gardens were dry and ignored. Yet there was a serenity in the inner dried up gardens with their waterless fountains. The crowds in the square outside seemed a long way off.

Kneeling on shabby mats, many Muslims were chanting and bowing on one side of the huge area under the dome of the Mosque. I could see another group of about 30 old men in earnest discussions further inside the Mosque. The Inmans, or leaders, were impressive with their long white beards and flowing robes.

While I was there, a principal Inman was being interviewed by a French newspaper correspondent. They were discussing the Chinese treatment of Muslim minorities. According to the correspondent and his wife, with whom I discussed the interview, Muslims had more freedom to worship than in previous years under Chinese rule, but religion was still controlled by the government. China had begun to treat the minorities better. But the government still suspected the Muslims because of their separatist motivations. However, the more serious problem to the indigenous religions was the huge influx of Han Chinese replacing the natives in businesses, jobs, farms and schools. To the locals, the immigration was genocide, since the policy would ultimately lead to the elimination of a culture, a race and a religion.

The interview was completed about the same time that the religious services were over. About 100 older men led by their tottering patriarchs came down the steps of the Mosque past me. They waved me out of the way, upset at my camera. It was a rare opportunity to me since, it was only in China and Turkey that I'd been allowed to view a service inside a Mosque. To the Muslims, freedom of religion includes the right to keep out nonbelievers, especially tourists with cameras.

Kashgar centered around the outside of the Mosque. As I stepped through the narrow gate from the Mosque onto the street the city burst upon my senses. There were innumerable people, shops, stalls and stores that produced a cacophony of noises and smells that assaulted one's senses. The movie theatre, not the Mosque, seemed to be the main attraction. The soundtrack from the movie then playing blared into the square. The people were lively and many were dressed in their traditional, colorful garments. Kashgar struck me as one continual county fair.

Probably the main Muslim tourist attraction in Kashgar was a well preserved monument to the dead on the outskirts of town, the Abakh Hoja Tomb. Although it was an imposing dome of tile filled with coffins and even mummies of a prominent Muslim missionary family, it seemed too quiet and depressed, the people dark and drab, particularly in light of the upbeat atmosphere of Kashgar itself.

Our second day in Kashgar was on Children's Day, a national celebration in China. The center of attraction for the day was to be at Kashgar's central park. While Keith was working with the equipment and getting Tang and Chuan's tent repaired, I went to the park.

To my surprise, the huge open green field surrounded by large buildings and an enormous statue of Mao Tse Tung was completely empty. The people were all walking to a smaller area and going through a gate.

I bought a ticket to go into the park behind the gate. Near the entrance, on both sides, were countless stands selling colored sugar water, candy, breads, cooked rice, and other edibles. I was not alone. Thousands were already there. The park was dirty and overcrowded. Once it

must have been a beautiful garden with trees, grass, watercourses, and a small lake. But in spite of the dirt and crowd it was a happy place. Everyone was in a holiday mood - picnickers, children running everywhere, hawkers selling food, lovers holding hands, nappers under the trees and families smiling and laughing. The Chinese children were very colorfully dressed for the occasion.

I walked back alone in the late afternoon to the hotel. In the lobby, in long rows were at least 30 modern "western" suitcases. "Tourists," I surmised and went on to the desk.

Then I backtracked, "Where did these people come from?" I asked myself. Since the lobby was deserted, I poked among the luggage reading the tags. To my amazement several showed San Francisco addresses. San Francisco was as far from Kashgar as one could go and still be on this planet.

I rushed to find the tour guide. She explained that this was an especially adventurous group from the San Francisco Bay Area and she invited me to join them at a special Mongolian banquet that night.

The banquet was overrated, but I bubbled with enthusiasm. I had always thought travelers who talked of nothing but home were a bore, but now I found it fun. They were somewhat interested in my adventures, but even more interested in telling me their own trials and tribulations.

One of the first tour groups allowed into Kashgar, they had flown in from Urumchi for a three day stay. My adventures and the questionable prospects for the next 2000 miles seemed minor to their fears of lost baggage, delayed plane flights, bad food, and dirty (or worse) hotel accommodations. Assuaging my own gnawing fears about the journey ahead, I

For the finale, the lights were dimmed... six buxom young women danced onto the stage...

enjoyed the comic relief that their anxieties created.

Until that evening I was unaware of how tired I had become of not being able to communicate without using pidgin English with the Chinese, or gesturing with the locals. The joy, and relief, of being able to talk to people normally was a shock. I didn't think it had mattered. Being with some fellow San Franciscans, if for only a moment, reminded me of the toll of loneliness that the road had taken. I had not expected great bonds of friendship with Keith, in fact I had not given the subject any thought, but I certainly did not anticipate what I got. So with my new friends there was much wine and laughter shared.

After the dinner they invited me to go with them in their bus downtown to a musical review. Held in a high school-like auditorium, the show was a cross between the 1950's and the 1350's. The result was a funny hodge podge of old rock and folk tunes, 1950's suits, ancient ethnic dresses, electronic guitars and shepherds flutes, jitterbug and native dance. It went on too long, but it was fun.

For the finale, the lights were dimmed. Soft rock blared out from the loudspeakers and six heavily made up, buxom young women danced onto the stage in very tight white jumpsuits to the sound of a heavy beat and immersed in flashing multi-colored lights. In my many trips all over puritanical China over the last six years I had never seen anything remotely as sexy as this.

This dance troupe (and probably the wine) convinced me that Fragrance, the legendary imperial Han concubine who lived in splendid garden isolation in Kashgar, was not just a legend after all. She had indeed passed on her charms to generations of progeny. While the veiled ladies in the town square may have inspired romantic fantasies of the Arabian Nights, these ladies inspired much less romantic and much more primal fantasies.

14 DECISION

It was time for me to go home.

In my heart I knew it. Tang and Chuan wished and schemed for it. And Keith saw it as a resolution to all his problems.

They had all said I would never get to Kashgar. Having proved them wrong, I could now leave "with honor"... Still a first, never done before, cycling through the Gobi, the Taklamaton Desert and over the Tian Shan Mountains, tracking by bicycle Marco Polo's 13th Century route through China, I had done it.

Although only two days were scheduled, we had actually spent four in Kashgar. Time had now run out. Our sojourn had worn thin. All the other travelers I had read about going through Central Asia had faced the same dilemma here - go forward or go home. Either way, Kashgar was the place of decision. Kashgar was a way point, not a destination, a place to pass through, not a place to stay.

Relieved of the daily stress of cycling, my thoughts had turned more and more towards home. Although I tried for hours, I couldn't complete a telephone call to California. The San Francisco tourists were returning to Urumchi the same day we were scheduled to leave by bicycle for the south. Their tour guide, Nancy Pickford, offered to arrange a ticket for me to go with them.

Just the thought of the 800 grueling miles behind us exhausted me. The next 2,200 miles ahead seemed unimaginable. Marco Polo, Sven Hedin, J.R.H. Foster, reported in their journals that the deserts and mountains south of Kashgar were more desolate, dangerous and difficult than any travelers had ever experienced before, "ascending mountain after mountain . . . and through valleys in perpetual succession, passing many rivers and endless desert tracks without seeing any habitation or the appearance of verdure. "Every article of provision must therefore be carried with you." And, as one of them said, "this land is a frightful picture of cold and desolation..."

My knowledge about the route to Tibet was not all based on reports of travelers centuries ago. Current maps and military reports showed we would have to cycle over some of the world's highest passes through areas without any paved roads and in some places with no roads at all. The area was also known for violent winds, snow, mud and sand - all an anathema to bicycle travel. We couldn't wait for the storms to stop or the snows to melt because of flooding in the valleys and, later, in Tibet.

Chuan reported conversations with PLA drivers in Kashgar which revealed that the "passes were unpassable," the valleys were "muddy," the weather was "terrible" and the armies "wanted more permits," before we could pass. He also told Keith that he was especially worried about me, since there were no medical facilities for 2,000 miles beyond Yarkant and "Alan won't make it one hundred miles in those mountains."

Although made physically more comfortable by rest, warm water in which to bathe, edible food and clean sheets, our expedition, as a group was no happier, especially about the overloaded van. Tang desperately feared a breakdown in the "terrible desolation" ahead. He demanded we hire another vehicle and I pay the $5,000 for it for the trip over the mountains to Tibet. He and Chuan had hoped the expedition wouldn't make it to Kashgar but now that we were here they were extremely anxious, fearing we might decide to go on. Because of me, the overloaded van and the impossibilities of the journey beyond, they argued we should return to Urumchi.

"We are already too late," Tang explained, "to get to Tibet before the snows melt." Our planned route through southern Tibet would become an impassable lake once the annual runoff began from the Himalayas in late June and July.

Keith was still irritated and unhappy with me because I had slowed the group down on the way to Kaskgar. He was going to proceed no matter what happened. He made it very clear that if he failed it would be because of me. I felt that I had been used just to lower his cost and now was considered disposable and could be sent home along with the other excess baggage. That made me so furious it clouded the realization that I had had enough of Central Asia anyway.

In the heated argument Keith and I had a week before I had agreed I would ride his daily quota of miles. If I couldn't do it, I would ride in the van and go home as soon as it was possible. Keith, who had his lap top computer in the van, then prepared a written day-by-day mileage quota, with specific rest days, all the way through to Lhasa. I was sure I couldn't ride the distance he insisted on each day, but I agreed and even signed his document after he conceded that any surplus mileage in any one day would be credited to the next. This wasn't total lunacy. I was getting stronger every day and had met the mileage quotas that last week before reaching Kashgar.

But Keith had insisted on thirty to sixty miles a day in our journey through three of the world's highest mountain ranges to Tibet. "That would have been good mileage for the van, let alone bicycling," I argued. But to no avail. I was sure this was a setup.

The extra time in Kashgar put us behind schedule. Although Keith wouldn't budge on the daily quotas, he did agree to a few more rest days and three more days at Mount Kailas.

I never hinted to Keith or Tang or Chuan that I was even thinking about going home. If they had known, they never would have let up on their pressure to get me to leave. Knowing, them, they would most likely have hustled me to the airport immediately and, if there was no room on the plane, strapped me and my bicycle to the wing... So, to keep them off guard, I heatedly joined in the arguments about whether we needed another vehicle and who would pay for it.

It was Tibet in general, and Mount Kailas in particular, that drew me on. "After all," I thought, "while 2,000 miles may be impossible, a few miles each day might not be, quotas, storms and snow notwithstanding." Furthermore, I was on a pilgrimage. Maybe there was a spiritual equivalent to "no pain, no gain." I decided to at least ride to Yarkant, an historic old road town southeast of Kashgar mentioned by all the ancient travelers. From Yarkant the road turns due south through the Pamirs, the Kun Lun and the Korakorum, all with imposing passes from 12,000 to 16,000 feet high.

In the meantime, Keith assuaged Tang by agreeing to jettison another mound of baggage. We abandoned more clothing, spare parts, food, equipment, film, etc., with the promise it would be shipped to Beijing and kept for us there. I didn't trust them with our borrowed Sony video camera and my Hasselblaad even though they had proved useless on the trip so far. As with the Urumchi and Korla offloadings we never saw any of it again. I do feel some satisfaction in thinking that our goods and chattel strewn all over a thousand miles of Central Asia will probably be used by the natives for generations to come. We spent almost a whole day sorting gear to abandon, packing, cleaning, repacking and writing letters. I took two baths, had two naps and ate four meals, gorging in such luxuries as if the next day was to be my last.

With the sky clear and blue, the morning of June 3rd was brilliant. The golden dawn bathed our hotel in beautiful light and I felt the confirmation of the previous nights dream - I was going on. I felt upbeat but a little anxious. Mount Kailas, the desert and the passes, the rivers and cliffs, the sun, the moon and stars, the long road south all whispered their call.

Nonetheless, there was a lump in my throat as I said goodbye to the San Francisco tour group as they boarded their air-conditioned bus for the Kashgar airport. With all the packing and repacking, we didn't leave the hotel until hours later in the afternoon.

While there was hesitation and vacillation at first, once it was resolved in my mind, I was comitted. "I will go on," became a reality, no less significant, no less unalterable than gravity. As with gravity, the further and higher I cycled into the mountains to the south, the more it became inevitable that I would be forced downward.

15 THE LONG CYCLE

It was our turn to leave. With the local CMA representative guiding us by truck, we headed on to the highway south towards Sachi. The well paved road was lined with poplar trees. A light, cooling breeze provided us with a rare tailwind.

After all the introspection and uncertainty, it felt good to be back on the road. We passed a large lake which exuded a cool, fresh smell. The Pamir Range to our right, crowned by Mt. Mustagata, "father of icebergs," rose in white majesty, bathed in the rays of the afternoon sun. Our mood was optimistic.

Suddenly the highway led up a sharp hill. We were back on the desert. Our plan was for a short ride - only 50 to 60 kilometers and then to make camp. Later in the afternoon the wind shifted against us and the skies to the west darkened. Keith and I cycled together to Yinahisha, a small village adjoining a huge army base under construction. We had completed our planned 60 kilometers and were very hungry. Our meal for the day was in the van which we hadn't seen for hours.

Keith and I kept pedaling thinking that the van was ahead. We ate every scrap of food we had in our saddle bags. Finally we stopped in the desert at Post 1595 figuring by then Tang would be looking for us and would eventually have to pass us. In the meantime the wind had increased and the sky grew darker. The temperature had dropped rapidly. We waited two and one half hours.

What we didn't know was that Tang and Chuan had stopped at the army base at Yinahisha after leaving us on the outskirts of Kashgar. They had stopped there to feast on a huge meal and didn't see us when we passed through the town.

When they finally drove up, Tang said, "The dark clouds in the mountains to the west mean rain and 'hurricane winds'." He adamantly refused to camp out as we had planned because the "tents would blow down." Even though I knew he and Chuan wanted to sabotage the journey and would say anything to keep from camping out, because of the radical change in the weather, I half believed the story about the hurricane. Keith was unsure about the weather and we were too tired to argue. It seemed far easier to pedal a little farther, not realizing we wouldn't see the van again for another 60 kilometers.

It was almost midnight when we finally reached Sachi. No hurricane. We found the van parked in front of a low complex of buildings and were ushered into a filthy hovel of a motel. There was only one small room available and it had only three beds.

Too exhausted to eat or complain I said I would sleep in the van. I climbed into the front seat with the baggage and tried to sleep. It was stifling and cramped. I was longer than the front seat was wide. Gnats and mosquitoes swarmed outside the closed windows so I didn't dare go out for anything or even open the windows.

Gnats and mosquitos swarmed
outside the closed windows of the van...

It was the furthest we had ever cycled in one day - about 225 kilometers. But even after only a few fitful hours of sleep, I still felt strong, ready for the dawn and the unknown tracks to the south.

The next morning we rode through pastures and irrigated fields to Yarkant. When we arrived we were escorted to a small, dirty bungalow in the center of town which was the CMA headquarters.

The local CMA chief had driven by jeep, several times, the next few hundred miles of our route south. He had gone as far as K-2, the world's second highest mountain. He said the road was too rough for bicycles, the passes still snowbound, the streams too full to cross and the altitude would deplete all our energy. He also refused to allow us to proceed without another vehicle.

"From here on there is nowhere to re-supply," he told us. "You'll have to carry all your food, drink and equipment - tents, bike parts, film, cameras and spare parts as well as gas to for the vehicle and even your water."

At that they all turned on me. They told me that without another van I would be risking all their lives. Because of my age, they said, I was the greatest risk. With only one van, if it or I broke down, it would be a disaster. Keith, Tang, and Chuan's point was that all of the journey's problems so far were "my fault," therefore I should pay for the additional vehicle and driver. I was livid with anger, yet I agreed.

Now that I look back, the only thing I felt was "my fault" was how I let them badger me into accepting that I was the cause of all the problems. For me this was not a unique incident. I remembered years ago I discovered that my wife was having an affair with her piano teacher. In the ensuing argument her rationale was that it was "all my fault." I was bitter, but I had let it pass.

I was brought up with the concept that I should always do my duty, behave honorably, and accept responsibility for my actions. There is nothing wrong with that, and I still believe it strongly. But my problem was that someone could take the most ludicrous premise, and if I was responsible in the most minute way, I would accept it as being my problem. It became easy to manipulate me into accepting all of the responsibility for everything that went wrong.

I was not the perfect husband, so I accepted the argument that I was somehow responsible for my wife having an affair. I got sick on this journey, so it was because of me that the expedition was behind schedule. I brought my own food, so it was my fault that the van was overloaded. I was so convinced of my responsibility for everything that it never occurred to me that the problems in any relationship are seldom, if ever, due to just one of the parties, that it was Keith who brought Amanda along preventing me from being able to take time to get adjusted to the cycling, and that if I hadn't brought my own food I would still have eaten, so the overall volume of supplies would not have been reduced.

Therefore, I agreed to pay the additional $1,300 (a mysterious major drop from the $5,000 quoted in Kashgar) for another driver and vehicle to travel with us from Yarkant to Shiqanha. I resented it, yet in retrospect maybe it was worth the price. It made me aware of how easily manipulated I was and served as a reminder that I have to truly review the facts of a given situation before simply giving in and then hating it afterwards.

Keith was now ecstatic because I could be made to ride if I slowed him down. Tang and Chuan were delighted that they had more cargo space and were able to use a "friend" of Tang's as the other driver. I seethed.

They had promised me that we would leave Yarkant immediately if I agreed to pay for the van, but they lied. We didn't leave the next day. So while Tang and Chuan were fussing with the new vehicle and additional supplies I wandered around the small town and explored the unpaved dirt road that we were to take. It disappeared into the foothills about 20 kilometers away.

16 INTO THE VOID

It took us two days to reach Kokyer, the last village for hundreds of miles. To say "village" is to be kind - a pile of dust would have been more correct.

The day, before we had gone about 70 kilometers and were 1000 feet higher than when we started. Our camp was made on a small plateau completely devoid of life. I looked but couldn't find so much as a blade of grass. The wind from the deserts to the north was intense. Our tents were almost blown away and if we had been on our bicycles it would have blown us up into the mountains.

After Kokyer we saw no one. The only thing that seemed to be here were rocks.

One day the road took us to a narrow, rock-bound valley - there was no way out visible in any direction. Coming around a curve I saw directly above us our first true mountain pass. The steep switchbacks wound higher and higher - straight up into the clouds. One look made me decide to pop a few of Dr. Rudy's high altitude vitamin and mineral supplements. Then, in my lowest gear, I proceeded.

The road had been blasted from the rock face of the mountain and was barely wide enough for a truck. The inside was a rock wall and on the outside a soft shoulder - no guardrail and a straight drop of hundreds of feet.

The first thing the driver and I noticed were each other's eyes.
He was shocked and I was terrified.

About a third of the way up, I looked up the road and saw my worst expectations fulfilled. A large army truck heading down towards me! Then I saw it wasn't just a single truck but an entire convoy. There wasn't enough room on the road for the truck and my bike. I hugged the rock wall on the inside of the road. The first thing the driver and I noticed were each other's eyes. He was shocked and I was terrified. The driver was wonderful! He cautiously pulled his huge truck all the way out on the soft outside shoulder. I was sure his rig would fall off the cliff. But he made it and smiled and waved at me. Each truck in the entire convoy did the same thing. I stood smiling, waving and shouting thank you's as each of them passed.

Nothing could stop me now. Diarrhea, treacherous roads, sore rear, shaky legs were ignored. After four hours I reached the top of the 9000 foot pass, well ahead of Keith, feeling euphoric and powerful. I then coasted down the other side jarred by the washboard bumps of the dirt road.

Coming up the other side of the pass was a heavily loaded caravan of about 20 camels. In some ways they seemed more dependable and were certainly more dramatic than the truck convoys. Camel caravans were used by the PLA in extremely rough terrain, at higher altitudes and in the worst weather where trucks could not be depended upon. This particular caravan was returning from supplying a climb on K-2, a hundred miles to the southwest.

At the bottom of the pass Tang tried to get us to cycle an extra 40 kilometers so we could stay that night at another army camp. "It's an easy ride and all downhill," he said. This time Keith was on my side - he didn't believe it was easy either. We made camp by a sparkling stream at least another 2000 feet higher than we were the night before.

A new enemy arrived. Cold. The temperatures were well below freezing. By this time I was wearing everything I could for warmth - gloves under my down gloves, wool cycling pants under my regular pants covered by another pair of wool pants, a wool shirt, wool sweater,

*Coming up the other side of the pass
was a heavily loaded camel caravan...*

and a heavy down jacket. But the cold still penetrated my gloves and even my layer upon
layer of clothes. With all those clothes I was a fat target for the wind. I was blown around
so much that I could not ride. So I got off and wheeled my bike up the muddy, icy track.
My hands ached and my face and ears were frostbitten. High rock cliffs hemmed in the road
keeping out any possible warmth from the rays of the sun.

This was but a taste of what lay ahead - Mazor Pass - our entrance to Kun Lun Shan, home
of some of the highest mountains in the world. Here were over 1000 miles of desolate
mountain ranges, from Pakistan on the west across Central Asia deep into China's Quinghai
Province on the east.

As I approached Mazor Pass the sun vanished behind huge white clouds that billowed in
from the south. The wind grew colder. The climb became very steep. With each switchback
there was an abrupt change in direction. The true pass was never in sight. I would drain
myself of every ounce of energy I had to reach what I thought was the pass. And each time I
thought I had reached the top I was faced with the agony of knowing that I had arrived at
only the start of a still higher climb. I bitterly gave Mazor it's own name - Two-Faced Pass.

Tang came by in the van, wheels spinning in the snow, and offered me a ride. It warmed me to see that he was genuinely concerned about me. But I waved him on. I was going to beat this pass myself no matter where the damn thing was. He seemed impressed with my resolve.

When I did reach the 13,000 foot pass it was alternately snowing and clearing - icy, windy and freezing cold. I put on even more clothes and gasped at the stunning view of the Kun Luns. They seemed endless, huge and now white mountains - rows and rows of them, dominating the earth forever. More foreboding and strikingly beautiful than any mountain range I had ever seen. Soon I was back on my bike and rode down the pass yelling my triumph over "Two-Faced Pass" unheeding the dangers of sailing 35 miles per hour down a dirt rock road not knowing what was around the next corner. In less than an hour and a half, exhausted, I reached the plateau below and the military crossroads at Mazor.

We cycled half a mile towards K-2 to enter the PLA camp. It was a group of low concrete buildings that were dingy and cold, but reasonably clean. We all ate in the mess hall at the commander's table. A rather rickety thing, but it was still an honor to dine at it since it was the only table in the place. The troops squatted on the cement floor to eat.

The base commander was most interested in and amazed by all the vitamins and minerals I was taking. He also told me, through Chuan, that Tang had reported I was very strong and had come over the pass with no trouble. I was terribly pleased with myself.

After dinner we were invited by the road construction crew at the base to share with them the first night of Ramadan, the Muslin holy season of fasting by day and feasting at night. The road crew, separate from the PLA, were primarily Uygurs and other indigenous peoples. They were all Muslims except for the top leadership. We walked to their camp about three-quarters of a mile from the base. I was flattered to be included in this celebration, held in a small room. There were about fifteen celebrants seated along the walls. A huge spread of food was laid out - cooked and fresh vegetables, breads, desserts, beer, rice, baked dishes, fish and many, many other exotic dishes. With my still questionable stomach, I ate very little, but I enjoyed the company and the beer. I was moved by the generosity of these Muslims who were so cheerful, friendly, and hospitable.

Around ll:00 p.m. I returned to the base and climbed into the front seat of "my van" to sleep. Since I paid for the second van I had taken to sleeping in it. I re-lived for a few moments the extraordinary effort of the past two days. What came to mind was how much I had envied other people's accomplishments. Now I felt just getting here was pretty spectacular. I thought, "If I catch myself envying others, I will look back on this and feel proud and envious no more." I was pleased.

17 SHANGHAI OF THE WEST

I could hardly believe we were getting close to Xiadulla. It seemed only yesterday that we had left Kashgar, or was it a thousand years ago? I had been on this road for 1700 miles. The passes were proving tiresome and endless - 10,000 feet, 12,000 feet, 15,000 feet no longer seemed fantastic.

We were ahead of schedule and it was Keith now who wanted to stop by 4:00 p.m. in the afternoon. There were even higher mountains ahead and I wanted to move on to "bank" a few days just in case we ran into difficulties. It was I who had become relentless and pushed on and on in growing determination.

I had energy to spare. An early stop gave me time to climb a ridge and look back on the days ride along a long, muddy shallow river valley. Here was a naked moonscape of sand, gravel and rock colored in reds, blacks, grays and browns. Looking back, I could see that beyond every bend was another bend, behind every hill another hill just like the one before. All that day, as I was riding up to each curve in the road, I strained to cycle around it to see what was next. To me this barren nothingness was beautiful.

The complaints and squabbles continued, but I shut them out of my mind. I shut them out so completely that I remember nothing about our second driver, not even his name. He may have been a very wise man deciding to remain invisible in the midst of our constant strife. I had given up trying to force Tang and Chuan to camp out. I no longer had any tolerance for Chuan who would lie, travel too far, or slow us down so that he could spend the night in some nauseatingly filthy army post. In exchange for my silence they were to bring me my food and water each day no later than noon. I usually began each days ride before dawn, by noon I had traveled three-quarters of the daily distance quota and was out of energy, food and water. It made me angry when they were late. Thus each days lunch drop became an irritant. An irritant that escalated the later they arrived.

One night, long after Keith and I were supposed to be asleep, Chuan and Tang opened the back door of "my van" and quietly removed expedition supplies. They then jammed them into the other van, intentionally overloading it. I couldn't figure out just what they were doing. It didn't make any sense for them to be moving things around in the middle of the night. I was troubled and uneasy again about just who they were. We were at their mercy out there.

Even with my suspicions aroused I could not help but notice the beauty of the night sky. This was truly incredible - brighter than any planetarium show I had ever seen. The stars crowded the sky, seemingly touching each other. Their brilliance seemed almost audible, as if the skies were humming some sacred mantra. I was awestruck.

The cold, isolation, and the tensions of the expedition were getting to everyone. The next morning offered a 3000 foot climb over 20 kilometers to a 17,210 foot pass over an unforgiving series of switchbacks on muddy roads. Even the downhill side was no joy. A storm was brewing, Tang and Chuan were late with my food again, the washboard bumps jarred my whole body, my rear was getting more sore. My arms and back ached from trying to control the bike. Even my hat was a foe. It kept falling over my eyes because of the wind and the bouncing of the bike. My bike seemed unhappy too - a little stiff and more difficult to control. We both needed adjusting, cleaning and repair.

I actually looked forward to the next army base stop at Xiadulla - literally meaning "30 mile camp." It was dubbed by the PLA as the Shanghai of the West, supposedly having clean beds, running water, new buildings and a big kitchen. More important to me was that our schedule called for a rest day there. I really needed that.

At the bottom of, by now, just another pass all I could see was the road to the south across a hard flat plain. Xiadulla was not in sight. It was further away than I had hoped.

A jeep load of well dressed PLA officers passed, stopped ahead of me and got out signaling me to stop. I was afraid they were going to create some sort of problem so I refused to stop and just rode on. They got back into their jeep and passed me in a cloud of dust. "Good riddance," I thought. Later I found out they were staff from Xiadulla who had come out to welcome me and give me a ride the last few miles. Clearly I was becoming burned-out by the journey.

When I arrived two hours later I was assigned a room to myself on the second floor of the concrete barracks. It was clean, had two beds, a wash basin, a thermos of hot water, and a fresh towel. As soon as I had finished giving myself a sponge bath with the thermos of hot water, in came in ten people - men and women, officers and enlisted personnel. Chuan wasn't there to translate and none of them spoke English, but they obviously wanted to communicate. I was starved for friendly interaction, so I was delighted with the role of host. I tried the best I could to explain all about our expedition with gestures. We had a great time.

Later, a doctor from the base hospital came by to talk. He knew a smattering of English, so that made the whole process a lot easier. He was concerned about my health at that altitude. I'm six feet tall, skinny, have completely white hair (I've had that since I was 35 years old), and had, at that point of the journey, a fairly long, scruffy white beard. I must have looked 150 years old. I could certainly understand why he would wonder about my health. It was an amazing coincidence that this doctor was doing research on coronary heart disease particularly lipid (blood fat) levels among active PLA troops at high altitudes. That was a parallel study to Drs. Farqhuar and Rudy's in which I was the guinea pig on this journey. Small world.

At Xiadulla I felt comfortable for the first time in a long, long time. Although we had agreed not to spend extra rest days here it snowed the morning we were to leave and no one wanted to go just yet. It was a good time to clean and repair our bikes and equipment, read and rest. Chuan said he was suffering from some sort of serious intestinal problem and was "ordered" to stay for a blood test. In the meantime I enjoyed playing ping pong and actually managed to beat one PLA orderly, but was then firmly trounced by everyone else.

In the afternoon, with chores behind us, the base hospital staff arranged a basketball game between us and them. Our hosts played well. They were rough and highly competitive, but handicapped by height and poor passing. Keith obviously hadn't played much but did all right. Chuan ("ill" as he was), Tang and I played very well. The game was held outside amid snow flurries. We had an audience of about 150 people. The expedition won 56 to 44.

After the game another one of the doctors came up to me, concerned, about whether he had to deal with my possible immanent collapse. It was kind of him, and I told him so, but I was actually feeling very good. This might have been another first - outdoor international basketball competition played at 15,000 feet.

The short respite from our constant bickering was just that - short. It was never clear exactly what was the nature of Chuan's illness. He never seemed sick. But he and Tang added this to their arsenal of arguments about why the expedition should stop now. Even with the additional truck they complained that both vehicles were overloaded, supplies were low, the army was refusing to give us more gas, PLA army base commanders would refuse to honor our permit, the roads were already blocked by snow and there were floods in Tibet. "We're

This might have been another first - outdoor international basketball competition played at 15,000 feet.

too late," Tang said in perfect English - confirming my suspicion that he always understood English and that his ignorance was some sort of ploy.

The new twist was that with Chuan "ill" and sanitation limited, all of us would become infected with what he had. I had had it with Chuan. He was always scheming as to how to sabotage the expedition, he was late with food, lazy, a constant complainer, making "errors" in translation so we would miss meeting and stopping locations, all of which generally worsened an already unpleasant situation. When I said that of course we couldn't risk Chuan's health "we'll send him back alone," - Tang wouldn't hear of it.

There was a party our last night. I was tired but I could have joined them. I was comfortable playing basketball with these people, but when it came to a social situation I was still too self-conscious and shy to want to take part. So I used the excuse of needing my rest for the next day to avoid joining the fun. That night my sleep was filled with an extraordinary panorama of dreams...

18 MOUNTAIN PASSAGE

My Xiadulla dreams were full of anxieties - missed planes, longings for home and anger about the journey. This adventure had become a daily exercise in masochism.

The food since we left Kashgar had been awful. Not simply because it tasted bad but because it did not provide the necessary nutrients for this type of physical effort. Our diet was primarily rice, army-made cookies, and canned pears. Occasionally there would be a bit of meat or canned vegetables. Without the food and supplements I had brought with me I would probably have collapsed.

The altitude was a problem too. I would wake up at night gasping for air. Even with the slow steady adjustment to those heights, each breath became an effort.

There had always been an ambiguity as to where the expedition would end. Originally Keith had said Chengdu, but we were denied permits to go there, so no firm decision had been made as to the new stopping place. My primary goal was Tibet and Mt. Kailas. That morning as we left Xiadulla, I decided I would go back to San Francisco when, and if, I reached Lhasa, Tibet. That's what I believed my dreams were telling me to do. I was ready to go home. I wanted to see my adult children, Alan, Jr., and Sharon. I wanted to see my mother again, and I was looking forward to that trip to Disneyworld with Shan. An imaginary synthetic Disney adventure in Florida sounded just wonderful.

However, I couldn't just tell Keith and the others I was going to leave when we reached Lhasa. That could be used as a bargaining chip to negotiate a few concession when I could really use them. After all, there were many more miles yet to be traveled.

Tang had told us the days ride from Xiadulla to the next army camp, Poerhtashih, would be easy - only 55 kilometers. He failed to mention the 16,900 foot pass on the way. The climb was so long, and gradual, I felt as if we had to cycle forever upward into the sky. When I finally reached the top, spread out below me was a large valley meadow surrounded by sharp snow capped peaks resembling the Grand Tetons in Idaho.

Long before Chuan and Tang caught up with us, Keith and I had passed Poerhtashih and were well ahead of schedule. I was pleased because it meant we would skip the army base and camp out. When they passed me in the van (over an hour late as usual), they said they would look for a camp site, but it had to have water since Chuan had forgotten to fill the huge plastic water containers back at Xiadulla. They disappeared over a ridge. By late afternoon, the van returned. "It's too windy, and we can't find water, so we will have to go back to Poerhtashih," Chuan explained, barely able to conceal his joy at not having to make camp. I was furious.

"Let's just camp here," I shouted.

"We can't without water, so we have to return to Poerhtashih quickly to be sure we can stay there," Chuan retorted as they drove off.

"Can there be no Holy Mountain,
can there be no Sacred Lake...
when the Lama smiles?"
Tregau Monastery, Tibet.

"Lamas come in all colors."
Author in a hot springs pool
on the road to Lhasa, Tibet

"Woe to those who do obeisance to the demons
of the sands, the rains, the snow..."
Expedition van crossing a river near Zongba, Tibet.

154

"For every prayer there is a flag, for every flag there is a prayer
for every soul whose body raises it to the Dolma La"
Prayer flags and Explorer Club flags at the 18,600 foot pass on Mt. Kailas.

"Let us gather together and
share our creature comforts."
Tibetan sheep in the Tsang Po Valley

"It's a narrow way to nirvana."
Tashilunpo Lamasary, Xigatse, Tibet.

"Beware of blankets bearing gifts: you -
to the resident bedbugs.
Four star motel on the road to Lhasa.

"Like the kings of Tibet, you become a corpse
when you cut your mountain rope, you connection to heaven."
Kangrimpoche, Tibet

"And the teacher on the mountain asked:
Why does Shiva live here?
Why does the Buddha govern here?
Why do we worship here?"
Rock face of the Holy Mountain in Western Tibet.

"Light in transition from day to night best illumes the soul."
Manasarovar the Sacred Lake at Mt. Kailas.

Unable to do anything about the situation, and just barely able to see the humor of having to go backwards - at least we hadn't done that before - we pedaled the 18 kilometers back of Poerhtashih.

Camp tensions had reached a new high. The dilapidation of the base defied description. Keith and I were both angry. The walls had collapsed around the base, every window was broken, and it seemed deserted. When we got to the center of the complex of broken down buildings, a small band of disheveled PLA members were making dinner on a dirt floor in a smoke filled room. The men just sat there in the smoke, barely looking up, and offering us nothing. They were obviously not pleased to see us. As for me, the feeling was mutual.

Keith proceeded to dress Chuan down for not bringing water. We both told him he was a danger to the group, a slacker, negligent and should leave. "It would be great for the rest of us," Keith said. Chuan now argued that it was the army's fault since they were stingy with their water - changing his previous admission that he had just forgotten.

The base commander refused to let foreigners sleep inside the base. Thank heaven for small favors. I slept in the van, Keith in the tent. Chuan and Tang slept inside the base they so much wanted to go to, on the dirt floors, along with a lively rat population. A small, but sweet, bit of revenge.

The next day, a 70 kilometer cycle, was the second time I arrived at camp before Keith, although we left at about the same time. The road was now so rutted and steep that I had been forced to walk my bike about 13 kilometers of the way. Keith had also began to adopt my schedule of beginning each day at first light.

It had become my habit to walk around our camp area taking pictures and enjoying the spectacular scenery as well as being alone. Of course I was alone all day too, but I wanted to avoid whatever the current camp conflict would be for the night. I got to bed early, ate by myself, and meditated.

The bitter cold was still with us. Once while going over a 16,000 foot pass my water bottle froze. I had nothing to drink for a four hour steep uphill climb. This pass did offer a very special ride down. There was no road, only truck tracks everywhere. We picked our own way in a "freefall" down the mountain. It came as close to flying on a bicycle as I would ever experience. The surface was sand that had been hardened into a crust by the sun and cold. This surface would support the bike as long as I didn't apply the brakes or turn too sharply. The surface was extremely smooth, I just let my bike go and soared down the steep slopes coasting to a stop on the plain below.

In spite of all the hardships, I loved the beauty of the area. The stunning turquoise lakes, the brilliant white ice and snow, and the light yellow grass were all magnificent. Nothing any of the others did ever diminished it. I was my own peace, my own liberation.

We had now cycled to an area claimed both by China and India. Almost 15,000 square miles of desolation called the Aksai Chin. It was completely barren, useless, extremely windy and mountainous, with an altitude range of 16,000 to 21,000 feet. Thousands of Indians and PLA soldiers died for this ground. The huge concrete bunkers, now abandoned, steel tank traps and ruined facilities built to support these armies were awesome. It was mind boggling to think that they were built by underdeveloped nations who at the time had insufficient capital or even the infrastructure to feed their own populations.

We were also passing through the Korakoram mountains, a very high range that began in Afghanistan and ran for over three hundred miles to the south and east through Hunza country, the Kashmir border and Ladakh, or Little Tibet, and along the disputed frontier of India and China. This area included the Aksai Chin, reputed to be the coldest place on earth. When we were there it certainly lived up to its reputation. The roads were so bumpy that it was easier to ride cross country on the crusted sand.

We were beginning to see animals along the southern border of this area, mountain goats and mountain sheep. I was so used to seeing nothing that they came as a surprise. At one camp Tang went hunting and came back with a rabbit. The stew of rabbit, rice, wild onions, and greens was so delicious I gorged myself.

The landscape was subtly changing. The passes were higher, some well over 17,000 foot, and there were more of them, but they seemed gentler. Everyday now we were cycling past lakes. The road became a mere track in the soft sand. As we headed south, I experienced a strange phenomena. I decided it was due to the Tibetan saint, Milarepa. After learning and misusing black magic, repented, and spent a lifetime as an ascetic.

In his later life, he became a teacher, advising that the road to nirvana was through asceticism, meditation and solitude. Here on my own painful journey, I realized I was living his tenents without knowing it. Alone each day I was, suffering physical hardship and trying to understand myself. The only book I brought on the journey was the songs of Milarepa.

As we came closer to Tibet and I thought more about Milarepa, an unusual phenomena began about 10:30 a.m. each day. By then I had been riding four or five hours, was getting sore, tired and hungry. Suddenly, especially if I was going uphill, everything became very easy. My breathing quieted down, the discomfort in my rear and legs disappeared , and I pumped faster - almost effortlessly. Everything seemed amusing and light, the world more beautiful, my anxieties forgotten, I was almost in a state of euphoria. This would last for about and hour and a half. It was eerie, but I liked it.

I wondered what caused it. Was it a mental aberration, self-hypnosis, or a spiritual experience? Accepting this "second wind" thankfully, I called it the Milarepa Effect.

My mood seemed to be changing along with the landscape. Everyday there was some new revelation of beauty - a lake transformed into gold by the sunrise for instance.

One day I had just come over a 17,200 foot pass to find myself at the edge of a lake glistening with tiny rainbows in the wind whipped waves. Standing spectacularly across the lake were two perfectly matched pyramid peaks, over 21,000 feet high, side by side with the early morning sun shining towards me directly from the space between them. One peak was entirely white, the other totally black. It was obvious from the broken beer bottle glass the truckers also stopped to stare. Even their garbage of glass added to the beauty. The bits and pieces sparkled in the sun as if someone had scattered emeralds, sapphires and peridot as offerings.

Where I stood were the ruins of an ancient temple. I could feel the awe and inspiration the scene must have given to the monks who lived here long ago in their temple by the lake. But I had come too late. I was saddened as if old friends had left, never to be seen again.

Although we were still cycling at over 16,000 feet the hills seemed more rolling, the weather a little warmer, the winds less devastating and the lakes and streams more plentiful. There was grass on the hillsides and more sheep. I began to feel more comfortable. Something had changed, I could feel it.

That afternoon, after making camp, I saw a tent about a mile away. I went over to investigate. A young man came to greet me. He showed me inside his large black tent. As soon as I saw him, I knew why I felt so at home. We were in Tibet.

19 FROM DIRT TO SUBLIME

My first morning in Tibet was a 28 kilometer joyride. Cool and sunny, a smooth road, all downhill, through flowered meadows beside a stream of clear water. We were to travel 70 kilometers that day. From our first Tibetan camp at over 16,000 feet to Nako Tso, a lake at 14,000 feet. Nako Tso was a huge deep body of water with interesting green and pale brown rocks reflected on its still surface. We camped beside it, washing our bikes and the vans in the cold water.

Conditions changed dramatically when the road came out of the meadow valley into a flat plain. It became very rough. There were ten inch high bumps every six inches in the road that shook me continuously. On one occasion the bumps jarred me loose from my bike and sent me sprawling. Another time I was catapulted over the front wheel when I hit a sandy spot that brought my bike, but not me, to an immediate standstill. It was impossible to avoid the bumps by cycling off the road because the sand was so deep and soft that the bike would simply sink.

Now and then Tibetans would appear, but, unlike the Chinese, they avoided us. A lone Tibetan "cowboy" dressed in traditional black garb with a high stovepipe hat was riding directly towards me, but when he saw me coming he turned off the road. Tibetans here are nomads and herders living in tents tending their herds of sheep, goats, and yaks.

Although we were losing altitude overall, except for a few high passes, the road was still difficult. The jagged rocks and impossibly deep sand made it tough to even walk my bike. Here was a noticeable increase in wild birds and animals. Left alone by Buddhist Tibetans who do not kill animals, geese and ducks abounded in the lakes and meadows. Stirred by the haunting calls of the geese as they flew overhead, I left a prayer flag at a mountain pass in their honor.

We left the lake early the following morning because Tang insisted we cycle over 90 kilometer a day. "The snows are melting in the Himalayas and we will be stuck in Tibet," he complained.

What he really wanted was to get to a supposedly fancy tourist hotel in Shiqanha. He went so far as to adjust the odometer in the van to decrease the mileage traveled so Keith and I would be deceived into thinking we weren't being pushed as much as we were. Tang actually passed two army posts so we could travel farther. The long rides over the difficult terrain were taking a substantial toll. Keith was weakening and was even more tired than I was.

One night, along this stretch of road, while I was searching the van for more film, I found a large number of enormous green rocks lining the floor. They were in a layer under our supplies and were covered by a tarp to hide them from sight. I didn't know what they were, so I told Keith about them. He looked and immediately identified them as chunks of jade. I later learned from Keith that Tang and Chuan had gathered the jade in the Kun Luns and were smuggling them using our expedition as a cover. We emptied out the van and threw the rocks away while Tang and Chuan were gone.

We also discovered that much of our food supplies was gone. The more expensive items such as the canned vegetables, meat and fish, had disappeared. Keith and I were able to piece together our separate bits of information about Tang and Chuan's movements and figured out they had sold the expedition's food supplies. That was the reason for the strange shifting of cargo in the middle of the night I had observed earlier.

We later realized how stupid we had been in throwing out the jade. Tang and Chuan could be very dangerous people. For our own safety we decided to say nothing and hoped they would blame each other for the disappearance of the jade.

A couple of days later, I spent hours photographing several Tibetans moving a flock of sheep from a high meadow down to the stream by our camp. Their black ten, with smoke rising from its center, was only about a hundred yards away from us. A woman from the tent came out every few minutes to check the progress of the flock, undoubtedly timing her dinner for her family's return. Their tent life, close family ties and dinner together seemed the perfect existence. Soon they would put away the black winter tent and make their home in a white, lighter, cooler and more rain resistant summer tent. I was soothed by the sense of rhythm and oneness with the land of their lives. It was a hard life, but one that was clean and pure and honest in sharp contrast to mine.

The mountains to the east were part of a new range called the Trans-Himalayas by Sven Hedin, a Swedish traveler and writer. Also known as the Gangdise Shan, the impressive range parallels the Himalayas through western Tibet. We were now within a few hundred miles of its highest peak, Mt. Kailas, my spiritual reason for the journey.

About a week after we entered Tibet we arrived in Shiqanha, China's western hub in Tibet. We stayed in Shiqanha's "finest" - a newly constructed concrete hotel complex. The rooms were spacious and clean. I was told that this town was being planned as a major tourist destination for western Tibet and that the hotel was part of the master plan. This seemed a bit odd in that there were no real roads to Shiqanha and there was no airport.

Possibly the hotel itself offered the best example as to why the tourist plan was doomed. There were a few Chinese guests but no Tibetans and no foreigners. The hotel stank. The place had large bathrooms, one for each wing of each floor, and the latest in modern plumbing. The reason for the terrible smell was evident after one visit to these modern bathrooms - nothing flushed. In fact, there was no running water at all, hot or cold. That explained the mystery of the large oil drums filled with water in the hallways, but not the one as to where to relieve oneself. That was solved when I went to the roof to take pictures of the town. The roof stank too. That proved to be the hotel's open-air toilet.

Another deterrent to tourism might be that there was absolutely nothing to see or do. It took about 40 minutes to walk around the entire town. There was a half deserted market with almost nothing for sale, and that was about it.

The most distinctive feature was the dust. It covered everyone and everything turning the entire place into an ugly monochromatic brown gray. I was very happy to leave the next morning in spite of the strong headwinds and crosswinds.

But before we left, the matter of our second vehicle had to be dealt with. The driver and the van had only been contracted to travel as far as Shiqanha and it was time for them to leave. The new point of dispute was how I was going to pay for the van. Chuan said the CMA demanded U.S. dollars in cash. I certainly didn't have $1,300 in cash on me. I hoped the impasse would delay payment until we reached Lhasa. But Tang then took me to the town's only bank to arrange to get U.S. dollars.

We were ushered into a small room. There facing me were more overstuffed chairs with doilies on them. Several bank officials were in the room, some giggling, some smiling, and some non-committal. They did have one thing in common, none of them spoke English.

After an hour of non-communications, Tang related to me that they would give me the cash if I gave them my traveler's checks.

Tang and I then took the cash to the CMA. Like any good consumer, I demanded a receipt. Tang refused to sign a receipt. I refused to turn over the money. In the ensuring argument, Tang's understanding of English again improved dramatically. He finally relented and signed the receipt, but only after writing in the statement that the extra van was "at my request." That was a blatant lie. The Chinese government may have approved our trip as a goodwill gesture, but Tang and Chuan and the assorted CMA officials along the route obviously had more personal and profitable motives.

Our road out of Shiqanha more or less followed the Indus River. One morning I picked a road to the right that led away from the Indus. After a mile or two, all truck tracks disappeared. I had not picked wisely. Tang and Chuan had not shown up and there was no sign of Keith. About two miles to the north I could see what looked like a newly built road on the other side. I went over to the river hoping to cross over to it. Not possible - the river was a raging torrent. About a mile upstream I could see a PLA truck stuck midstream with water flowing over it's hood and two tractors trying to winch it to the other side. Just then I saw Keith on the road across the river.

The river was roaring too loudly for me to hear anything, but Keith gestured to me to cross it. I knew I couldn't at that point so I followed the river downstream, but it dead-ended into the village of Gar. For centuries Gar was an oft mentioned first stop as an entrance to Tibet. But it had been passed by in modern times and now contained only a few run down houses, many ruined structures and no indication that this was ever once a major trading center. With sign language and a map I tried to explain to the local people that I needed to cross the river. No one understood even though they were trying hard to be helpful.

I finally decided to start over and cycle back to the fork in the road. An hour later Keith appeared. He had found out he too was on the wrong road. Tang and Chuan had gone ahead almost 60 kilometers without seeing either of us, so they doubled back and we were together again.

At our camp that evening a few Tibetans appeared and joined us. They accepted our offer of a Chinese Coke, then proceeded to pour out the contents onto the ground, and walked away with their treasure - the bottle.

I had taken to sleeping out in the open without my tent. The sky was bright with the light of a glorious full moon. I slept better than I had since the trip began. Every now and then I even overslept.

My spirits rose with every mile closer to Mt. Kailas. Our last army camp before reaching the mountain was the sub-camp of Garyassa at Muchi. Although I had wanted to go on, Tang and Chuan once again deceived us into staying by telling us we had gone further than we really had. Until I checked the odometer I thought to myself that I must have been having a permanent Milarepa Effect and was flying instead of cycling our daily mileage. I felt so positive about getting to Mt. Kailas that I just wasn't angry anymore.

Finally the day came that I had thought about about for over 2000 miles. It began in the dark overcast predawn. I left before anyone was awake. In the dim light I followed truck tracks and telephone poles to a high ridge, then into a divide between two mountains. Afraid that I was getting lost, I stopped and asked the mountain to guide me. That soothed my nerves and I decided to retrace my route. A few minutes later a line of stone markers to the south appeared. There was no road and I wondered why anyone would build markers here if they had no meaning. I followed them and within two miles I came out onto the main road.

The weather had deteriorated. After coming over the last pass from the west into the Kailas/Lake Manasarovar basin, I knew the mountain was only a few miles away behind the foreboding clouds to the east. The clouds darkened and the skies were punctuated with thunder and lightning. It began to hail, lightly at first, then in large pellets. I got off my bike and put on my rain jacket and pants in time to avoid getting wet. Comfortably warm and shielded from the sting of the hail stones, I sat down in the desert with my back to the wind and my face towards Kangrimpoche (the Tibetan name for the mountain).

For a few moments the storm lifted. There was Kangrimpoche facing me - almost standing over me - higher than I remembered and pure dazzling white. The hail stopped. The veil of the storm covered the mountain again. I sat transfixed.

20 MOUNTAIN OF LIFE

While Mt. Kailas is not known to most Westerners, it is to many eastern religions, including Hindu, Buddhism, Jains and Bonpos, the "meru" or center of the world. It is the mythical mountain, the connecting link between earth and heaven, and the home of Shiva - a major god of India.

In my readings about religions of the Far East I had been intrigued by the legends surrounding Kailas. I had become lost on the mountain during an earlier visit and credit my rescue as almost a re-birth. There are places on earth people regard as sacred, supernatural or other worldly. While I cannot explain it, there is a different feeling at Kailas.

* * *

All four of the great rivers that flow into the Indian sub-continent have their source within 75 miles of where I sat. The Indus River's source is to the north, known as Senge Khambab, "the river coming out of the mouth of a lion" to Tibetans. From the east comes the Tsang Po or Tamcho Khambab, "river coming our of the mouth of a horse." From the west flows the Sutlej or Lengchen Khambab, "river coming out of the mouth of an elephant." And from the south the Karnali or Mapcha Khambab, "river coming out of the mouth of a peacock." These rivers have sustained the civilizations of what is now Tibet, Bangladesh, India, Nepal and Kashmir for thousands of years.

Tibetan legends say that in ancient times Tibet was a vast ocean surrounded by forests. Five gigantic poisonous dragons lived in this vast ocean and their stirrings created huge waves. The waves began to destroy all of the vegetation. Sensing a catastrophe, the animals and birds were terrified. Rose colored clouds then appeared over the waters. These clouds were transformed into supernatural beings who subdued the dragons and calmed the sea. "Stay with us forever," begged the animals. So the five beings commanded the ocean to withdraw. They turned the east into forests, the south into gardens, the north into grazing lands and the west into guards for the sacred mountains. These beings then became the five sacred peaks of Tibet, and at their center was Mt. Kailas.

The ancient myth that the Himalayas and Tibet were once an ocean is now an accepted scientific fact. The *Himalayan ichthyosaurus* lived 180 million years ago in the depths of this ocean. Over 30 feet long, their pointed noses made them efficient mollusk eaters. Over the eons the seas receded and continued geologic activity pushed what were once huge marshes into the highest mountains in the world. The clouds here, often rose colored at dusk, seem to lend truth of the Tibetan version of geology. And who is to say that the *Himalayan ichthyosaurus* wasn't a dragon... Besides, the Tibetan version is more fun.

According to legend, after the waters of the sea had receded, before there were human beings, a huge female ogre lived among the rocks and valley. She was frightful and heaped her vengeance and hate on all the animals - killing, maiming, and terrifying them. The animals pleaded for deliverance. The Bodhisatdttva of Mercy, later called Avalokitesara by the Buddhists, and Chenrisi by the Tibetans, sent a god to earth in the form of a monkey to

Five gigantic poisionous dragons lived in this vast ocean.

relieve the distress of the living creatures. Rather than engage the ogre in battle, the monkey made love to her. Their offspring were six baby monkeys who multiplied into five hundred. They ate the fruits of the trees and the wild grains in an earthly paradise. In time their tails became short, they learned to speak, and became human beings. This rather remarkably parallels the scientific concept of human evolution.

The Tibetans go on to say that after the dawn of man things were going badly on earth since there was no leader. The Sky God felt obligated to send one of his sons to earth to help. This was in thanks for the help that men had given him in his contest with a demon. This son's mother was a deity of the watery depths of the earth. When the molten power of the inner earth is combined with the sky the result is a sacred mountain - a thing that guides the winds and waters and weather and shows man the way.

Tibet's first king, Nyatri Tsenpo, came down from heaven by way of Mt. Kailas. For eons the kings and saints of Tibet came from heaven down this mountain. They always kept their "dmer," the rope connecting them to heaven. Trigium, a god in human form and son of the last of the Seven Thrones, fought a duel at Mt. Kailas with nine paternal and three maternal clans. During this battle his "dmer" was cut. So he became the first king to leave a corpse. From then on the tombs of kings were called mountains, the place of origin that touches the sky.

Shenrap Miwo, the patron saint of Bonpo, came to earth on "mu" the sacred mountain ladder of Kangrimpoche (Mt. Kailas). Bonpo, considered Tibet's indigenous religion, had a common heritage with Hindu and Shivaite. Bonpo's influence spread throughout Tibet from the Kyunglung region near Kailas.

Mt. Kailas is also the object of worship and pilgrimage for Hindus, Buddhists and Jains. This is extraordinary since Kailas is on the other side of the Himalayas from India and could only be reached by a tortuous route over the world's highest mountain range. According to Hindu sacred literature, a pilgrimage to "the Land of the Snows of Gods" and the sight of Mt. Kailas would transform the pilgrim into a vidyahhara, a super human gifted with special knowledge and understanding of the mystic worlds.

It was also at Kailas that Buddhism, the ultimate spiritual reality for Tibet, took hold. A contest between Bonpo and Buddhism is said to have taken place at Kangrimpoche. Padma Sambhava, the saint who brought Buddhism to Tibet, challenged a Bonpo priest to a duel which was to prove, through magic, ingenuity, and physical feats, which religion was more powerful. The last part of the challenge was a race around and a climb up to the summit of Kangrimpoche by the time the morning sun gilded the peak. The winner would possess the mountain and control the spiritual fate of Tibet.

The Bonpo began to climb while Padma Sambhava took a nap. Before dawn the Bonpo was almost to the top. Padma Sambhava waited until sunrise and rode on a sunbeam to the peak. When the Bonpo looked up and saw his rival, he was so shocked he fell down the slope, losing his prayer drum. Padma Sambhava adopted the drum as his own and used it to accompany his song of triumph.

Tibet as we think of it was founded by the 5th Dalai Lama, Songtsen Gamo, who united the country in the 7th century. He and his reincarnated successors, including the current 14th Dalai Lama, are believed to be imbued with the soul of Aralokiteshvara, the patron deity of Tibet. Aralokiteshvara has many arms with which to lead others to the mountain of nirvana. It was Songtsen Gampo who began construction of the Potala, home of the God Kings, and his capital.

Except for military forays into China as far as Xian, and into India, Angolia and Medoc, Tibet has made it a policy to isolate itself from the rest of the world. Tibet forbade all foreigners and non-Buddhists from visiting Mt. Kailas. The only exceptions were Indians, holy men, and pilgrims. It was believed that the prohibitions were for the good of the non-believers, since it was written that those who came to the mountain for a reason other than a true pilgrimage would return broken men.

The British invasion of Tibet in 1904 did not penetrate as far as Kailas. China never had any real presence in the area until long after their 1949 invasion and the flight of the 14th Dalai Lama into India. China in turn forbade all foreigners to travel to Mt. Kailas until the 1980's when a limited number of Indian pilgrims and tourists were admitted. In the year before this journey I was one of the few Westerners to visit Mt. Kailas.

* * *

I had fallen asleep at the base of the mountain. By the time the wind and the roar of thunder woke me from my nap it was late afternoon. Dark clouds still swirled around the mountain, but it had cleared to the east and I could see where I had been the year before. Memories of that first journey here came to mind...

* * *

I remembered being so pleased with myself for having obtained a permit to fly to Lhasa. I also remembered how shocked I was because, for the first few days, I had problems simply walking due to the high altitude. After trying for about a week I was able to get the Chinese tourist agency to take me to Kailas. Permission was only to look at the mountain. I could not spend the night there nor could I spend any time actually on the mountain.

Kailas is over 800 miles from Lhasa by way of roadless tracks that none of the Chinese tourist groups ever traveled. I had arrived late in the afternoon at the small building at the base of the mountain. Mt. Kailas was stunning. I was not expected. The Tibetan manager of the area, a man named Dorji, who was fluent in Tibetan, English and Chinese, said there was no room and my tourist agency escorts and that I could not stay there. Since it was late, he did agree to allow them to put up a tent for me, saying they could stay with some Tibetans who were there. Beyond the building were the tents of a few Tibetan pilgrims. My driver promised that we would leave very early the next morning to return to Lhasa. Dorji made it clear that I was to take no pictures, since they were forbidden.

I just could not let the opportunity pass to experience Mt. Kailas at closer range. When I crawled into my tent I had already decided I would wait until everyone was asleep and go for the mountain. After midnight I slipped out, climbed over the wall surrounding the compound, and got clear of the area without waking the dogs.

I was very pleased with myself until I realized I didn't know where to go. I had a flashlight but was afraid of using it. I headed straight up the road between the pilgrims' tents directly toward the mountain. I could see a gap in the rocks that looked like a trail and went towards it.

When I was within 75 yards of the gap, a dog lunged at me, barking viciously. I threw rocks and flashed my light at it to keep it at bay. I was very afraid of being arrested or bitten. I started to walk quickly and then run. My chest was pounding both because of my nervousness and the altitude.

Suddenly three more dogs started barking at me from another direction. I sat down, tried to take deep breaths, and kept the dogs off by shining my light in their eyes and throwing rocks at them. They quieted down if I stopped moving.

Realizing it would be impossible to return to the compound without being discovered, I found a road heading to my right and decided to following it in the hopes that the dogs would leave. As I half walked and half ran, the dogs left one by one. Still shaking, I climbed up a ridge to get my bearings and to sit and wait for the dawn. A short while later I noticed small lights proceeding along the trail. I surmised that these must be pilgrims getting an early start and decided to follow them.

It was an unusual and eerie experience to circumambulate Mt. Kailas, to follow the route used by pilgrims for over 2000 years. By afternoon, I was in a valley where the trail began over the highest pass, the 18,000 feet Dolma La. On the trail I met a small Tibetan group, a man, his wife, their child, and a very old man. They were very friendly and allowed me to follow them up the trail. They obviously knew where they were going. They were extremely hospitable and the young man insisted on carrying my pack for me. Even so it was hard for me to keep up since I was very tired and we were going steadily upwards. The old man led. When we arrived at an area with huge blocks of stone, each with a special mythical significance, the Tibetans took off their packs and sat down.

By now it was about 6:30 p.m. I assumed they were planning to stay the night. I sat down too. They offered me some barley and we ate some of the nuts and dried fruit I was carrying. Then the old man got up, put on his pack and continued up the path, breaking a trail through the snow. The young man was going to carry the child, so he returned my pack to me. They left and I tried to follow. They kept getting further and further away from me. It was starting to turn dark. They would occasionally look back, but they didn't wait for me.

The snow flurries increased, and it was becoming impossible to find their footsteps in the snow. With each moment I was left further behind.

Far above, they stopped at the top of the pass and looked down at me for a moment, turned, and disappeared. I panicked and plunged upwards through the snow. I thought I saw a small stone shelter on the pass, and decided to climb the rest of the way and spend the night in it.

When I reached the 18,600 foot pass my clothes were wet with sweat and my face, arms and hands were becoming frostbitten. It was now dark. I was desperately thirsty. My mouth was so dry I could not even eat the snow. The wind blew snow flurries around me. The thing that I thought was a stone shelter was nothing more than a huge boulder draped with prayer flags flapping in the wind. The snow storm had obliterated the trail. I was too tired to walk any further.

I wrapped my coat as tightly as I could around myself and laid down. My feet were freezing so I tried to take off my boots and put on dry socks. But they were frozen and I didn't have the strength to get my boots off. I used my extra socks as gloves. I began to shiver. I knew shivering was dangerous. I tried to stop by consciously relaxing and trying to meditate away the cold. It would work for a short while; then I would doze off and wake with a start, out of breath and gasping for air. I would then begin to shiver all over again.

I accepted the fact that I was going to die. This actually seemed to calm me and I shivered less. It was clear that this was going to be a classic case of mountain death. I had violated all the rules of mountaineering - I was alone, had no equipment, was inadequately dressed, and in poor physical condition for the climb.

I told myself I would fight to survive as long as I could. I prayed. After a time the first of my miracles occurred. The snow storm stopped, the wind died down, and the sky cleared leaving only a huge full moon in the sky. I took that to be a sign that I would survive.

I must have dozed off again because my next memory was the gray light of predawn. Soon the rays of the sun were shining on the pass. I tried to get up, but was too tired, stiff and weak. My mouth was still so dry there wasn't enough saliva to suck snow or eat the food I had with me.

The sun had been up about half an hour when two Tibetans appeared from the south. They were Bonpo pilgrims since they had been circling the mountain counterclockwise, the Bonpo route. It was my second miracle of the mountain. In the first place Bonpo pilgrims are rare, and secondly there were very few pilgrims at Kailas at that time of the year. How on earth did they just happen to come upon me?

The two took one look at me and knew exactly what to do. They didn't say a word, made a yak dung fire, melted snow for me to drink, and gave me some of their tsampa (parched barley flour). The warmth of the fire, the hot water along with the food rejuvenated me. I wanted to cry but couldn't. I thanked them profusely and offered them what I had, but they refused.

Without so much as a word, they left down the pass heading north. I never saw them again.

21 THE PILGRIMAGE

The thoughts of my last night on the mountain and the storm on the Dolma La aroused me from my reverie. I realized I had been sitting there for two hours. Dusk was approaching. It was still several miles to Dorchen, Dorji's compound. I didn't know where Tang planned for us to spend the night, so I headed for Dorchen.

After a couple of miles a wide fast moving, but shallow, stream blocked the road. A Tibetan camp was nearby. I went over, and in answer to my inquiry, they said they had not seen the van or Keith. As I walked out of their white tent, I saw Keith and the van coming upstream towards me.

We peddled together to Dorchen and set up camp near Dorji's compound. Since Tibetans do not fish, trout swarmed in the streams and could literally be picked up. Tang did some hand fishing and we enjoyed a huge fish dinner. We had allocated five or six days at the "holy ice mountain" and the "unconquerable lake" at its base.

Dorji was not there when we arrived, but when we met the next morning we hugged as old, old friends. Although I had violated his rule the year before against going on the mountain,

I had been forgiven. Knowing of my strong interest, he offered to take me to Milarepa's home, a cave in the mountain. It was only a few miles away on the pilgrimage trail if we went counterclockwise. Circling the mountain to the cave clockwise would have been a two day 30 mile trip.

Dorji said, "I don't have time to go around the whole mountain with you. But I need to visit the Lama at the cave to be sure he is all right. Do you mind going the Bonpo way?"

"No, I want to circle the mountain counterclockwise as homage to the Bonpos who saved me last year," I replied.

Dorji seemed pleased with my answer. Besides my heavy pack, all that marred our walk was my concern about Dorji's health. He was pale and coughed often. He said he was fine but told me the monk at Milarepa's cave was very ill and had been unable to walk the past year. We decided to give him my vitamins hoping they might be of help. Dorji remarked how much better I looked this time as compared to last year.

To Tibetans natural objects are souls of people, beings unto themselves, or homes for gods or demons. As we walked along Dorji told me stories about all of them. It seemed every nook and cranny, every rock, and even parts of the trail itself had its own story.

I was tired. The backpack was heavy, but because of my last experience I wasn't traveling light. I carried my tent, a large sleeping bag, extra clothing and enough food for several days.

Dorji led me off the trail to a very small rebuilt gompa (temple) constructed around Milarepa's cave. Only one old Lama lived there. He was the last surviving Lama of what had once been a large monastery catering to pilgrims who circled the mountain. The Chinese Red Guards in the 1960's had destroyed the monastery building as well as all of its contents. It was but one of 6,252 monasteries destroyed by them.

The Lama was grateful for the vitamins and offered us tea. He answered my question about why Milarepa was called the Laughing Saint. Through Dorji, he said, "Milarepa was a devil in his early life and caused much suffering and weeping and changed so much in one lifetime that he became a saint. If one thinks about that long enough, it is worth laughing about."

Through Dorji he also told me that Milarepa and other highly developed Lamas could leave their bodies and return, maintain luminous meditations with sleep, observe, direct and abolish dreams, enter into the "rainbow body" that was indestructible, engage in mind transference, take over a newly dead body and maintain consciousness with a light technique, completely free of thought whether asleep or awake. Milarepa, he noted, had said the mountain was a place to practice for the Guru or Yogi to obtain the absolute, the emptiness and to experience the phenomena of spirit. He added that salvation and liberation came from years of practice, asceticism, meditation and solitude. It could also come from sudden illumination that could occur after a cathartic event.

Dorji added that the mountain will develop the skills of enlightenment which are possessed by everyone. He said meditation is a technique of realization and climbing the mountain pass is an experimental demonstration of the absolute or true reality or realization of the spirit within.

Dorji said good-bye after I made him accept a bottle of vitamins. He disappeared over the hill to Dorchen. Because there was no room for me to sleep at the gompa, I scrambled up the cliff above and found a ledge wide enough to lay out my sleeping bag. Afraid that I would roll off the ledge in my sleep, I didn't rest well. But the beauty of the night sky more than made up for the loss.

In the morning I continued around the mountain. The hike up to the Dolma La was hard because of my pack. Several Tibetan pilgrims met me coming the other way. They tried to tell me that I was going the wrong way. I replied, "Bonpo, Bonpo." They would laugh, then let me pass.

Word had apparently spread to everyone on the mountain that I had met the Dalai Lama, their God King. I met with him several years before on a trip of Dharamsala, India, where he currently resides. We had a picture taken together and I brought it with me. A picture of the Dalai Lama is highly prized by Tibetans and forbidden by the Chinese. I brought a number of copies. Every pilgrim I met that afternoon asked for one.

The Dolma La itself was less foreboding this time even though it was cold and overcast. I buried a time capsule there with letter from Shan and his schoolmates. They had agreed that whoever got to Mt. Kailas first would dig it up and bring it back. I took photos to show them where to find it.

That night, I camped facing the gigantic east fact of Mt. Kailas. After a morning hike to touch the east face, I returned to Dorchen.

Keith was waiting for me. Unaware of any problem, I greeted him bubbling over with enthusiasm. However, he was angry. Just as I arrived, he was leaving for two days on the mountain. He said I was a whole day late, so he had sent Tang and Chuan to Barga, not to return for two days. He assumed I was going to circle the mountain in a day. That is physically possible - but not for me. "If I was a day late," I asked, "why didn't you send out someone to see if something had happened to me?" He didn't reply except to announce that there was no time now for me to walk around Lake Manasarovar and we would be leaving for Lhasa in two days.

Circumambulating Lake Manasarovar, the second part of a true pilgrimage to Mt. Kailas was vital to me. It would take at least three days to cover the 65 miles. Two days was just not enough time especially if I had to bike to Barga first. It was Keith's revenge for my late return. I told him so and he stormed out of the tent.

I was very upset but I looked forward to the extra two days on the mountain. They actually were wonderful. There was a gompa and a lake near the west face of Kailas a few miles from Dorchen I wanted to visit. Dorji told me to follow the stream to reach the gompa, and beyond the small lake. Pilgrims are not allowed to visit that lake until they have made thirteen trips around the mountain.

After about three hours of a steady, steep uphill climb, I came to the ruins of a small gompa which had been destroyed by the Red Guards. The thoroughness of this destruction was truly astounding. Prior to the scourge, the Lamas had all been ordered by the Chinese army to return to their home villages. Most of them complied and were then imprisoned or murdered. The Lamas who did not return to their home villages met the same fate, and were also imprisoned or murdered and their monasteries destroyed and looted.

According to Tibetan teachings, it is not so much the destruction of the monasteries or artifacts that would bring cosmic retribution, but the Chinese economic development of Tibet, their misuse of Tibet's resources and the destruction of its fragile environment. The Tibetans believe if one disturbed the ecosystem the gods would become angry.

It never ceases to amaze me that our extremely technologically sophisticated culture seems to come to the same conclusions as the Tibetans have without the benefit of all sorts of research and enviromental impact reports. We have much to learn from these people.

Following the stream to the gompa ruins, I discovered a huge natural amphitheater hemmed in by cliffs the most spectacular of which was a 2000 foot black rock wall that went straight up to the peak of Mt. Kailas. Every sound not only echoed but was amplified in this rock cathedral. Although the day began with bright sunshine, a sudden hail storm hit. There were loud howling noises - like that of wolves. I felt uneasy and uncomfortable. No wonder so much of the mysteries of Tibet were centered at this mountain. Feeling that I did not belong there, I left.

The Indians at Dorji's compound invited me to dinner that night. Rice, mushroom and a tsampa of barley and yak cheese was the menu for the evening. The night ended perfectly in Dorji's very small room, cozy and permeated with the smell of incense, lit only by one candle. His mother, who stayed with him in an even smaller adjoining room, served yak tea.

My pilgrimage was still incomplete. I had to circle Lake Manasarovar. Returning from his trip to the mountain and anxious to move on, Keith decided that since Tang and Chuan had not returned as planned, we should ride our bikes to the Barga army base. We agreed that he would leave the next day for Lhasa, but I would be permitted two days at the lake and then catch up with him and Tang and Chuan.

Since I only had two days to go around the lake, I left that same afternoon by bike for Hore, a village on the shore of the lake to begin my pilgrimage on foot. The sand and lack of roads made riding around the lake impossible. Hore was a depressed, small, dirty, mud village. It was an unhappy mixture of a few Tibetans and more Chinese. I needed a room for the night, food and a safe place to leave my bicycle. A large, greasy Tibetan signaled me to follow him through a door partly pulled off its hinges into a small, dark, dirty room. It had a dirt floor, a wide bench for a bed, a broken window, and indrescribably filthy blankets. The place also appeared to be a lice heaven. I had nowhere else to go so I resigned myself to the accommodations. My host and innkeeper then raised two fingers. I thought he meant two nights so I raised one finger, knowing I just couldn't wait to be gone as the next morning as soon as possible. He mistook my signal and thought I was bargaining on the price of the room. He was angry, but agreed to one yuan for the night before I could explain that two yuan was just fine with me. Eating there was beyond question, so I ate what I had with me.

The next project was how to keep my bike safe while I was gone. A young Tibetan man, better dressed than the others, speaking some English, offered to store the bike in his locker granary. He inspired confidence, so I arranged to leave it with him.

The extremely ill humor of the village struck me as artificial. As if there was something going on that I was not aware of - a feeling that I represented something no one wanted to be associated with. Possibly the local economy was in such a state of distress that no one had any spirit left with which to be hospitable. There was no doubt that I was some sort of villain.

As I was about to unscrew the small light bulb in the ceiling of my room (there were no light switches), the broken door opened. The young Tibetan who was storing my bike came in. He handed me ten yuans, "For your trip. You have to pay at the monastery at the end of the lake."

"I have money, but thank you. You are very kind," I told him.

He still insisted, "No money for room." He held up two fingers. I then realized he must have heard that I negotiated the price of the room from two yuan to one and concluded I must have been too poor to pay the going rate. He put the ten yuan on my bed and walked out into the night. That ten yuan has always been the most precious of gifts to me.

Awake with the first light, I paid the man who had showed me the room two yuan instead of one. He seemed pleased.

Walking around the lake proved to be difficult. At times I was plowing through the sand or tip-toeing on large stones along the shore. Because of the cliffs, there was sometimes no shore at all and I had to walk a few hundred yards inland. There were also times when I had to wade or swim across deep lagoon, marshes or stream inlets. I was sure there was a trail somewhere, but I never found it.

It was not until late afternoon that I reached Tregau which was being rebuilt. There were a few primitive rooms for the workers and another area for the resident Lama. They had several tents for visitors and pilgrims. There were foam pads for mattresses and clean blankets. The alter in the center room was not yet finished nor were there the usual spiritual trappings. I met the Lama and gave him one of my Dalai Lama pictures. He placed it on the altar of the chapel.

He then led me down some stairs into a dark underground room. It smelled smoky. A young girl took me by the hand and led me to a bench with a rug on it. That was the gompa's kitchen. They gave me a bowl of goulash. As they were watching me with interest, I didn't want to offend by refusing their offering. The food came from a boiling pot, so I thought it would be safe to eat. Besides, I was very hungry. The goulash was another version of tsamba. It was bitter and had sort of a urine taste. Aside from that, it was just fine.

Emerging from the dungeon kitchen, I saw the last lights of a bright red sun half sunken into the western horizon. The billowing pink clouds to the north near the holy mountain, and the snows which had been transformed into a brilliant gold color, were all reflected in the calm blue water of Lake Manasarovar.

I so wanted to stay at Tregau for a while, but I knew I had over 30 miles to hike the next day. Up again before even the first light of dawn, I began my walk along the lake's edge. The day was beautiful, hot with a light breeze and a few clouds. There were many steams to cross. At first I took off my shoes to avoid having to walk in wet footwear - I already had several blisters. But there were just too many streams for me to bother after a while and I waded with just my tennis shoes, but without socks. On the north end of the lake was a small barracks and a meeting room for Indian pilgrims. Just as I arrived, two vans drove up with about twenty pilgrims. From a distance I observed them perform their rituals to Shiva, blowing conch shells, lighting incense and immersing themselves in the lake.

I continued walking for miles. Then out of nowhere Tang appeared with the van. He said he had been looking for me all day. I enjoyed the ride to Barga and we had a wonderful dinner that night of duck, fish, rice, beans and PLA beer.

I was content to sleep in a storeroom on an army cot. In spite of the blisters on my feet, my pilgrimage had been a success. As I fell asleep, my only thought was, "I am happy."

Shangri La is a real place.

22 TIBET EXPRESS

I had done what I had set out to do. There were still over 1400 kilometers (800 miles) to Lhasa, 1400 kilometers to savor my success, to enjoy Tibet, to anticipate home, and to try to discover what was to come next for me. There were to be more miles of sand, mud, steep passes, floods, conflicts and possibly injury or sickness. But right now I looked forward to each day, undaunted and with pleasure. In that spirit, on a gray, rainy day we left Barga to catch up with Keith.

These last few hundred miles were in sharp contrast to our beginnings. I was healthy and much stronger. I had even become a bit of a "cyclist." I was more stoic. I did not dwell on what a long way 1400 kilometers really was by bicycle. "Enjoy the first pedal and the long journey will take care of itself," had become my daily motto.

For the first 3000 kilometers of the journey, the problems were thirst and dehydration. Towards the end, the biggest obstacle was water. The snows of the Himalayas were starting to melt and the floods were beginning.

We followed the Tsang Po watershed for hundreds of kilometers, crossing its tributaries many times. One false step in its roaring waters and we would have ended up floating down to the

Indian Ocean 2000 miles away. The Tsang Po begins near Mt. Kailas and flows the length of Tibet, almost completely around the Himalayas, into Bangladesh.

The rivers and steams swelled in the afternoons and evenings when the sun had melted the snow and ice in the mountains. We had to wait until morning, after the coldness of the night refroze the water, to make our crossings. On one occasion the van stalled midstream. Just as the water was rising, and we were rolling down the windows to "abandon ship," the van started.

Our last river crossing before Zongba, a regional headquarters in southwestern Tibet, was the most difficult. The year before I was able to cross that same section of river on a bridge. The bridge was a work of art - its steel superstructure was painted an incredibly bright sky blue which could be seen for miles, incongruous amid the desolate landscape, standing alone across the wide river. There were no roads approaching the bridge. Drivers would just see it from a distance and head towards it on their own route across the rocky desert. The bridge was essential because here the river ran fast and deep. But this time when I got to it the on-ramp had been washed away and the main roadway planks were missing.

Tang drove downstream to where the river broadened and seemed shallower. Here we decided to attempt to ford it. He drove cautiously into the river. All went well until the truck sank into a hole. Tang got excited, gunned the engine and turned upstream. The van stuck.

We all got out into the water in an effort to lighten the load. That didn't help a bit. The spinning rear wheels only dug themselves deeper into the hole. We then emptied the van by carrying everything to the other bank. Still the van wouldn't budge. Tang and Keith rigged up an elaborate belay, with a winch hooked to icepicks, on the shore. That only bent the picks and snapped the rope.

By this time we were all soaked and shivering. Dusk settled in. Afraid we would lose the vehicle as the water rose, I decided the only way to get out was to dig the van free of the rocks and mud under the water. I yelled, "Tang, get in and start up the engine. Chuan and Keith, get behind and push!"

I dug furiously at the rocks and mud around the left rear tire which had sunk deepest into the water. At first the van moved about a foot. With wheels spinning, it sank back into the hole. I dug faster and harder and yelled at Keith and Chuan to push harder. I signalled Tang to rev the engine as fast as it would go.

The engine roared. Tang shoved it into gear. The van began to move slowly out of the hole. With the extra push from Keith, Chuan and me, Tang got it free of the hole and drove to the other side. We all cheered.

Beyond Zongba, the rivers were bridged but we were deluged in rain. I felt like "superman." It didn't bother me, but my companions got so sick of the wet that we stayed inside for two days at Lhaze. Lhaze was an army camp on the main road from Lhasa to Nepal and a connecting link between the population centers of Tibet. Later, if we hadn't found a detour along an embankment that still held the raging, brown waters of the Bainang, we would have spent an extra week waiting for the rain to stop so they could re-open the only bridge.

The journey confirmed my love affair with the outdoors - no matter how difficult or unpleasant it could be. As I cycled across Tibet, the memories of difficult times began to fade. The whole adventure had become a kaleidoscope of changes in terrain, light, cultures and even colors.

While on the road between Zongba and Lhaze, we camped below "Hot Springs Pass." As we came over a ridge towards a sacred place in the foothills, on the downslope was an inferno. Geysers exploded water and steam with a loud hiss seventy feet into the air. Boiling pools bubbled sulfur gas. For a half a mile streams and pools of hot water covered the hillside from the road down to a small freshwater stream below.

It was a wonder of nature - a smorgasbord of bathtubs. They were hotter or cooler depending on their distance from the underground source. There were pools large enough to paddle around in and pools small enough to just fit into. Close to the cold stream below we could go for a refreshing cooling dip or up high to the ridge for an unusual view. We could also choose long hot streams where we could dig our own personal mud baths in the slope, or a hot water grotto surrounded by volcanic rocks.

I tried a number of different pools. I even washed my clothes in the hot water. Keith picked a pool on the other side of the stream. That may have been wise, for a Tibetan yak trader let his yak wander off while staring at me - undoubtedly his first sight of a naked white man.

The entire area was clean of the usual broken glass and debris. Prayer flags attested to the fact the people here considered this open air bath a cathedral.

As we left this valley of steam, several Tibetans deluged me with requests for pictures of the Dalai Lama. In gratitude I gave one to the caretaker of the area. I also gave one to a very old woman who offered me an entire brick of tea in exchange. I let her keep her tea. And one to a young man who had offered to guide us earlier in the day. Nature asked only respect for the hot springs, not compensation, for her gift of comfort and relaxation.

It had been many years since I had been so isolated for so long. This adventure had been a practice in solitude. It became apparent how people-fatigued I had become. On this last leg of the journey, my basic enjoyment of people had reasserted itself.

I could laugh along with the two women construction workers on "Rain Cloud Pass" who stopped me, apparently just to giggle at the odd sight of me. It was fun to sing along with a road crew, their haunting, non-melodic, off-key songs. They joined me in a version of *Home On The Range.* I also had a great time lunching in the pouring rain with a crew trying to repair a washed out road below Xigatse. All of us were laughing while Tang, Chuan and Keith sat miserably in the van.

Even the tourists were pleasant. Once we were on the main road to Lhasa we began to come into contact with more people.

I enjoyed the Brazilian tour group in our hotel in Xigatse. Tibet's second largest city, it contains the largest operating monastery, Tashilhunpo, home of the Panchen Lama, who is second only to the Dalai Lama. The Brazilians offered to let me join their group, but I had already been around the town. They berated their Chinese guide for telling them they were "two minutes late." "We are not Swiss," they said. "We go where and when we want."

Along the way all sorts of people seemed to become aware of my suitcase of medicines and vitamins. Such as an American woman, hitchhiking to Gyangze, Tibet's third largest city, who asked me to give her something for her "stomach flu." I gave her some of the antibiotics I had, but mostly I advised her to go home. She later took that advice and passed me in the back of an open truck headed for Lhasa.

He probably didn't have much of a chance, but I gave all the information I could to a young American planning to live off the land and ride his homemade covered wagon all the way to Kailas. I was also happy to tell my story to a well informed Tibetan who was trying to write a tourist guide to Tibet. He spoke excellent English, which made the task much easier for me.

Only the Tibetans seemed to suffer from the inter-relationships, not so much with tourists, but with the Chinese. They resented the Chinese occupation and felt all the educational and job opportunities were taken by the Chinese immigrants. They feared the systematic destruction of their culture and religion. They feared not just the desecration of their temples but the pollution of the air, water and land. Opposed to taking life of any kind, they were appalled at the wanton destruction, and in some places, the elimination of wild game and birds. They were concerned that Tibet had become a dumping ground for Chinese nuclear waste and the pressure to overgraze their land was so damaging to Tibet's fragile ecosystem that it was in danger of collapsing. They were not alone. The Uygurs in the Xinjiang Region had the same complaints.

Tibetans also had dreams of a future with the return of the Dalai Lama. They wanted to participate moderately, but still be able to retain their own culture and religion, in the modernization that China was trying to bring about.

More and more Tibetans were taking their pilgrimages to Kailas by truck over a few days, rather than by walking, which could take months. It seemed a tragedy that what had been a slow process of enjoying the land, the monasteries, and a time for personal reflection had turned into a "quickie" experience.

The indigenous peoples seemed most resentful in the large cities and administrative headquarters where there were large numbers of Chinese. These native peoples felt themselves superior to the immigrant Chinese, yet understood they had become an underclass.

Our last stop on the road to Lhasa was supposed to be an army camp near Ta-Lung. It turned out to have been abandoned by the army, but was being run as a motel with a bar. It was the first time we had seen a drinking establishment during the entire journey. We were all put into the same cold, dirty concrete room, probably once a barracks day room. My cot was by a window looking out into a huge courtyard. As I was looking out, there were two Tibetans women in tight, western skirts and low-cut blouses, staggering across the open area with Tibetan men in tow. They all appeared drunk. Their loud, slurred speech was no longer audible when they closed the door to a small room. It reminded me that here, happening before my eyes, was a repeat of the terrible tragedy of the Native American. Beautiful, complex, sophisticated cultures, allowed to flower in isolation, being forever destroyed. It saddened me.

The road from Kailas to Lhasa was an important time for me. No longer anxious, it was a time to be in touch with the best within. We ran out of food and existed for the last ten or twelve days on Chinese Coke and old army cookies. The result of the "disappearance" of our food supplies earlier in the trip. Even with the lack of adequate food, I continued to marvel at the beauty. There were new paths, valleys, streams and meadows - an endless panorama of new discoveries.

With my awareness of beauty was so heightened, I can now recall a vision I had of an idyllic scene. The road was smooth and slightly downhill, I was spinning along almost effortlessly. I saw a small village, several hundred yards from the road, with two streams coming down from the mountains and opening up onto green fields. High up, facing south, was a small gompa. The sun had magically lit the scene so that the greens of the fields and trees, the pastels of the village and the blue of the clear sky were breathtaking. Soon I was around the next curve in the road. It was gone. But I will always know, Shangri La is a real place.

Beauty was found not just in nature. It was in the people too - the Lama at Tregau, the man who gave me the ride up Dry Valley Pass, the tour guide in Kashgar, the doctor at Xiadulla, the old Uygur poet who read to me on the road near Aksu, Dorji and the old man I met at the fort at Gyangze.

Gyangze may be Tibet's third largest city, but here "third largest" means it can be covered in about forty minutes of exploration. But it is also a place rich in history.

I walked to the old fort on the hill overlooking the town. Scaling its crest, I tried to find a way to get inside to explore. An old man walked up the path. He reminded me of a Lama, but he wasn't dressed that way. For a yuan he opened the gate and gave me a tour of this "impregnable" fortress that the British commander, Colonel Francis Younghusband, had destroyed in 1904 in a few hours of bombing. The surviving 14th century murals, only partially destroyed by the Red Guards, and several temple rooms with Buddhist relics, altars, murals and intricate wood carvings of the Pantheon of Tantric Buddhist Gods and Special Beings were extraordinary. He showed me rooms within rooms, secret passageways and honeycombs of natural and man-made defenses, walls and fortifications. He told me, with tears in his eyes, about the losses from the bombardment by the British and the destruction by the Red Guards. He explained what had happened, showing me remnants of these battles, shrapnel and bullets, swords and spears.

Towards the end of the tour, he took me up steep rock stairs to the top of the fort, still scarred by the bombardment of 1904. There he shared the desperation, the loss, and the sadness of the last Tibetan troops who stood on this point. They knew that their flintlocks and swords were no match for the machine guns and bombs that came whistling in on the fort. Their bravery had not been enough to save their beloved homeland. It was here, overwhelmed by grief, that they hurled themselves over the parapet, several hundred feet to the rocks below to their death.

Our last days ride into Lhasa capsulized every cycling day we had experienced for three months. We crossed two long, steep passes - one over the shoulder of another sacred mountain with an imposing glacier right by the road and the other up from Yang-Cho-Yung, a huge lake with innumerable bays and inlets. On several occasions trucks or jeeps stopped and the drivers offered me a ride. I declined.

On our last pass it suddenly began raining and snowing at the same time. Without stopping to put on my rain gear or extra sweater, I followed Keith down the pass. The road was muddy and slick. Soon I was very cold and wet. It was too late to put on more clothes, so I

They hurled themselves over the parapet, several hundred feet to the rocks below to their death.

rode as fast as I could to the Kyi-Chu River, 3000 feet down from the top of the pass. I could see the sun was shining there.

Once I was into Lhasa Valley I was warm and dry. My spirits were high. The last kilometers to Lhasa were on a perfect road which was even paved for the last five kilometers.

When I rode into Lhasa, Keith, Tang and Chuan welcomed me with firecrackers and beer. Everyone seemed happy. An expedition first.

And we stayed that way. I spent two days in Lhasa at a hotel run by an American chain, revisiting some of my favorite places - the Potala - official home of the God King Dalai Lama in exile, the Jokang - Tibet's huge central temple, the Dalai Lama's summer palace, the park and the Sera Monastery.

Then it was over and I was on the plane to Chengdu. From Chengdu I continued on to Beijing and re-traced my route home.

Again I was at San Francisco International Airport where I had left for Asia three months before. Not only was I fifteen pounds lighter, but I was down to one duffle bag, my camera, film and bicycle. I wanted to savor the journey for a while and had no desire to see anyone except my family. The long plane trip from Lhasa gave me the chance for personal and cultural decompression. Sharon, my daughter, and my mother met me as I came out of customs. It was a perfect beginning for my return.

Later that afternoon, I went to the day camp he was attending to pick up my son. He seemed taller. He didn't recognize me. After all the other children left, he came out and looked around but didn't pay any attention to a gaunt man, with long, white hair and a huge beard. Unsure about the strange looking person in the hall, he turned the other way and got a drink from the water fountain. I just waited. He looked up again. "Dad!" he shouted and came running. I picked him up in my arms. I was happy... again. It had become a habit.

Epilogue

My good-byes in Lhasa were hurried. I bid farewell to Keith in the hotel lobby as I rushed to the airport. And to Tang and Chuan at the airport in the midst of the usual struggle to check in to an overbooked flight to Chengdu. Tang waved as he drove the van back towards Lhasa. I never found out exactly what he and Chuan's real purposes were on the journey, but, we still made it all the way. I never saw them again.

A month after my return Keith telephoned and after that we exchanged letters once. Keith had tried running from Lhasa to China. But gave up after three days, and returned to Lhasa in the van. He then rode his bike on the highway from Lhasa to China's Quinchi Province with Tang and Chuan following in the van. Keith's goals were to lead expeditions and then to live in a monastery. I've not heard from him since, though I suspect our paths may cross again someday.

Before returning to our regular household routine, Shan and I luxuriated for a week in Florida hotels with clean sheets and towels, water you could drink, and varieties of safely edible food. We visited Disneyworld, Epcot Center and the Kennedy Space Center. Then on to a few days in New York with my other son, Alan, Jr., who was attending Colombia Business School, and Jennifer, the lovely young lady who would soon become his wife.

Less than two weeks from my ride down the last pass, I was back at my desk at the law office, on the telephone, dictating, meeting with clients, managing, and telling "cycle stories" to anyone who would listen.

While I had not really expected any sort of catharsis, I was a little disappointed in how things had more or less just settled back into the same old routine. What I didn't notice right away was that there were major changes, but they were subtle. Just as I did not dwell on the pains of the journey, I was now able to let go some of the pains of my domestic failures, conflict, anger and estrangements. To me the journey had been worth the risk.

Six months after my return I met Nancy. We fell in love and married a year later. Even though we lived only three miles from each other, I would write to her and expected written responses. I was still unable to trust so that I wanted her words on paper as a verification. I have lapses occasionally, but with her I have experienced the new joys of shared intimacy and growth. With Nancy's help I again ran for public

208

office against a corrupt political machine. I lost. But rather than feeling that it was a personal failure, I felt good about the fact that I said what I felt needed to be said. I did the best I could and that is success.

I still travel, but no longer for escape. Now it is to share, to learn, and simply to enjoy. Nancy and I climbed Mt. Ararat on our honeymoon. If God chose to have Noah start over again from there, so could I.

There are also inner journeys. Without Nancy this book would never have been published. I had been so closed, that to share, even lightly manner, how I really felt about things, could not have been possible. Our joined families, her sons Christopher and McCabe, and my Shan, now all teenagers, continue to grow, adjust and learn - sometimes a difficult process.

My absorption with the spiritual aspects of Mt. Kailas have not made me a mystic or a Buddhist, Bonpo, Jain, or Hindu. In any event the Tantric Buddhism of Tibet is beyond my comprehension, my cultural heritage. I know there is much truth in the 108 books of Kanjur, the words of Buddha. And at least I know what they mean as to the three great vices - ignorance, hatred and lust, or the usefulness of reason to destroy false appearances but not to destroy intuition or spirit. We can all benefit from their respect for all life and all nature.

In what had been an unconscious preparation for my journey, I had travelled on other trips to sacred mountains all over Asia, especially surrounding Tibet - in India, Ladakh, Kashmir, Sikkim, Nepal, and China. Neither this journey nor those travels or my studies of comparative religions have captured my spiritual allegiance. They all have my appreciation.

Similarly, my appreciation of Islam and the many other religions of Central Asia have not made me a true believer. But all of them have shown me, and continue to provide, truths and new understandings.

Like Christianity and Judaism, all the sacred literatures and belief systems tell us we must not neglect the spiritual part of ourselves. In Kailasan terms, we must never sever our "dmer," our rope to heaven, that part of ourselves that connects us to our spirituality.

I kept a dream log almost every night of the journey. At home my dreams for weeks returned to Central Asia, with all the hidden desires, distortions, emotional predictions and even esoteric symbology of dreams. Thirteen days after my return, I dreamed of an old woman, a combined figure of Dorji's mother and my own grandmother who handed me a gift of a single block letter, a white "B." It was windy and I was afraid they would be blown away.

My analysis was the wind represented the headwinds in the snow white passes of the Kun Lun and the dangerous Dolma La, the "B" both the Buddhist cave in Toulapon and my Bonpo rescuers. The gift, the opposite of theft, related to the possessions I felt had been stolen when we off-loaded the van. Also the Bonpos, the "B," gave me the gift of life. And I was aware the gift must be put to good use. I will try.

Although still recognizing coincidences and luck, I have become more impressed with cause and effect, the touchstone of both science and religion. My travels to Asia, my meeting with Keith in Hong Kong, the ride up the Tian Shan, the Dolma La, the escapes from rain, snow, being lost and being sick, in that context gave my journey new meaning.

Personally I don't always see the differences in me from my experiences along the Silk Route and through Tibet. Others have. Some say that true personal change must be gradual and almost unrecognizable to oneself but obvious to friends and even acquaintances. The journey never would have happened had I not ardently believed we can master ourselves, we can understand and change if need be, we can be open to new experiences even new lives and new loves without destroying ourselves. Nancy and the journey proved that.

In retrospect there was no real difference between the road from Urumchi to Tibet and the road across Tibet. The road conditions, the terrain, the weather, the personal conflicts, were different, but in their own ways equally difficult, equally dangerous, equally challenging. There was one great difference. Me. My attitude. My feelings. My condition, physically, mentally, emotionally and spiritually. In all those ways I was different, positive, happy, strong, at peace, joyful.

While other people and circumstances do govern our lives, we can govern our own reactions to those circumstances and people, positive or negative, with humor or anger, love or hate, envy or support, suspicious or trusting.

We all see the world as we want to see it. The afterglow of the journey burns in me still. Every day I feel it, see it, remember it. Most of what I recall is that it was beautiful - beautiful all the way from Urumchi to Lhasa.

Index

Bibliography

Ai Li. *Qiuci Murals of Music and Dances.* The Xinjiang People's Publishing House, 1984.

Allen, Charles. *A Mountain in Tibet.* London: Futura Macdonald & Co., 1983.

Andres, Roy Chapman. *Across Mongolian Plains.* New York: Blue Ribbon Books, 1921.

Bernstein, Jeremy. "A Journey to Lhasa." *New Yorker.* Dec. 14, 1987, pp. 47-105.

Bueler, William. *Mountains of the World.* Seattle: The Mountaineers, 1977.

Cronin, Edward W., Jr. *The Arun.* Boston: Houghton Mifflin Co., 1971.

Evans-Wentz, W.Y. *The Sacred Mountain.* Chicago: Swallow Press, 1981.

Fleming, Peter. *News From Tartary.* London: Macdonald Futura Publishers, Ltd., 1980.

Fremantle, Francesca and Trungpa, Chogyam. *The Tibetan Book of the Dead.* Boulder: Shambhala, 1975.

Garside, Evelyne. *China Companion.* New York: Farrar, Straus, Giroux, 1981.

Harrer, Henrich. *Seven Years in Tibet.* London: Pan Books, Ltd., 1953.

Hassnain, F.M., Oki, Masato, and Sumi, Tokan D. *Ladakh: The Moonland*. New Delhi: Light and Life Publishers, 1977.

Hedin, Sven. *Trans-Himalaya, Vol. I & II*. London: MacMillan and Co., Ltd., 1909.

Hedin, Sven. *Trans-Himalaya, Vol. III*. London: MacMillan and Co., Ltd., 1913.

Hedin, Sven. *The Silk Road*. New York: E.P. Dutton & Co., Inc., 1938.

Hesse, Herman. *Siddhartha*. New York: New Directions Publishings, 1951.

Hopkirk, Peter. *Trespassers on the Roof of the World*. Los Angeles: J.P. Tarcher, Inc. 1983.

Kane, Robert, S. *Asia A to Z*. Garden City: Doubleday & Co., 1953.

Kawaguchi, Ekai. *Three Years in Tibet*. London: Theosophical Publishing Society, 1909.

Kublin, Hyman. *China Selected Readings*. Boston: Houghton Mifflin Company, 1968.

Lai, T.C. *Kweilin*. Hong Kong: Kelly & Walsh Ltd., 1976.

Landor, A. Henry Savage. *In the Forbidden Land, Vol. I & II*. New York: Harper & Brothers, 1899.

Lapiere, Richard. *Son of Han*. New York: Harper & Brothers, 1937.

Lhalungpa, Lobsang. *Tibet The Sacred Realm Photographs 1880-1950*. Philadelphia: Aperture, Inc., 1983.

Lukan, Karl. *Mountain Adventures*. London: Collins Publishers - Franklin Watts, Inc., 1972.

McElduff, Colin. *Trans-Asia Motoring*. London: Wilton House Gentry, 1976.

McGovern, William M. *The Early Empires of Central Asia*. Chapel Hill: University of North Carolina Press, 1939.

Polo, Marco. *Travels of Marco Polo.* London: Dorset Press, 1908.

Richardson, Hugh M. *Tibet and It's History.* Boulder: Shambhala, 1984.

Rossab, Morris. *Khubliai Khan.* Berkeley: University of California Press, 1988.

Sanderson, Ivan T. *Abominable Snowmen: Legend Come to Life.* Philadelphia: Chilton Company, 1961.

Shaw, Robert. *Visits to High Tartary, Yarkand and Kashgar.* Hong Kong: Oxford University Press, 1984.

Snelling, John. *The Sacred Mountain.* London: East West Publications, 1983.

Stein, M. Aurel. *Ruins of Desert Cathay.* London: MacMillan & Co., Ltd., 1912.

Stein, R.A. *Tibetan Civilization.* Palo Alto: Stanford University Press, 1972.

Tenzing, Norgay. *After Everest.* New Delhi: Vikas Publishing House, 1977.

Waddell, L. Augustine. *Tibetan Buddhism.* New York: Dover Publications, 1972.